All About Mount Kilimanjaro: A Kid's Guide to Africa's Tallest Mountain

Educational Books For Kids, Volume 46

Shah Rukh

Published by Shah Rukh, 2024.

While every precaution has been taken in the preparation of this book, the publisher assumes no responsibility for errors or omissions, or for damages resulting from the use of the information contained herein.

ALL ABOUT MOUNT KILIMANJARO: A KID'S GUIDE TO AFRICA'S TALLEST MOUNTAIN

First edition. November 6, 2024.

Copyright © 2024 Shah Rukh.

ISBN: 979-8224455157

Written by Shah Rukh.

Table of Contents

Prologue 1
Chapter 1: The Mighty Peak of Africa 2
Chapter 2: How Mount Kilimanjaro Was Formed 5
Chapter 3: The Great Glaciers on Top 8
Chapter 4: Unique Animals of the Mountain 11
Chapter 5: Plants and Forests of Kilimanjaro 15
Chapter 6: The People Who Live Near the Mountain 19
Chapter 7: Early Explorers and Adventurers 24
Chapter 8: Stories and Legends of Kilimanjaro 28
Chapter 9: Climbing the Mountain: What It Takes 33
Chapter 10: Famous Climbers and Their Journeys 37
Chapter 11: Different Routes Up Kilimanjaro 41
Chapter 12: Weather on the Mountain: From Hot to Freezing ... 46
Chapter 13: The Amazing Views from the Summit 50
Chapter 14: Life at the Base of the Mountain 54
Chapter 15: How Scientists Study Kilimanjaro 58
Chapter 16: The Effects of Climate Change on Kilimanjaro ... 63
Chapter 17: Safeguarding the Mountain for the Future 68
Chapter 18: Wildlife Conservation on the Slopes 73
Chapter 19: Fun Facts About Kilimanjaro 78
Chapter 20: How Kids Can Help Protect Mountains 83
Epilogue 88

Prologue

Welcome to the adventure of a lifetime! Have you ever imagined what it would be like to stand on top of the tallest mountain in Africa? Mount Kilimanjaro, with its snow-capped peak towering high above the plains, is not just any mountain. It's a place full of mystery, wonder, and stories waiting to be discovered.

In this book, you'll embark on a journey to learn all about Kilimanjaro's amazing features, from its icy glaciers and lush rainforests to the unique animals that call it home. You'll meet brave explorers who first conquered its heights, discover the secrets hidden in its legends, and find out what it takes to climb all the way to its summit. But that's not all—this book will also show you how people and scientists work together to protect this natural wonder and what you can do to help preserve mountains like Kilimanjaro.

So, get ready to dive into a world where nature's beauty meets epic adventures. Whether you dream of climbing to the top one day or simply want to learn more about this majestic giant, you're about to uncover the magic of Mount Kilimanjaro. Let the adventure begin!

Chapter 1: The Mighty Peak of Africa

Mount Kilimanjaro, known as the "Mighty Peak of Africa," is not only the tallest mountain in Africa but also one of the most remarkable peaks in the world. Standing at about 19,341 feet high, Kilimanjaro reaches toward the sky, almost like it's trying to touch the clouds. Its summit is called "Uhuru Peak," which means "freedom" in Swahili, a language spoken in the region. People from all around the globe travel to Tanzania, the country where Kilimanjaro is located, to see its majestic beauty up close. The mountain is part of a national park, protected to preserve its natural wonder and the many plants and animals that live on and around it.

What makes Kilimanjaro unique is that it isn't a typical mountain made up of hard rock alone. Kilimanjaro is actually a volcano! But don't worry; this volcano has been dormant for thousands of years, which means it hasn't erupted in a very long time and is considered safe for people to climb. The mountain has three volcanic cones, named Kibo, Mawenzi, and Shira. Kibo is the tallest cone and the one with Uhuru Peak at the top, while Mawenzi and Shira are shorter. Shira is actually an extinct volcano, which means it will never erupt again. Mawenzi is also extinct, but Kibo is dormant, meaning it's "asleep" and could technically erupt someday, though that's very unlikely.

One of the most amazing things about Kilimanjaro is how diverse its environment is. As you go higher up the mountain, the landscape and weather change dramatically. At the bottom, the base of Kilimanjaro is surrounded by green rainforests filled with tall trees, colorful flowers, and animals like monkeys, birds, and even elephants. It's warm and humid here, with plenty of rain to keep the forest lush and alive. As you climb a little higher, the rainforest begins to fade, and you enter a grassy area called the heath zone. This region is filled with shrubs, smaller trees, and giant plants that look like they belong in a fantasy world. Some plants in this area can grow as tall as a person, even though they're technically still part of the "shrubs" family!

Climbing even higher, the air starts to get cooler and thinner because there's less oxygen the closer you get to the top. The next zone you reach is called the alpine desert. Here, there are hardly any plants, and the ground is rocky and dry, almost like a desert in the sky. It's a challenging environment, with strong winds and harsh sunlight during the day, while at night, temperatures can drop below freezing. Despite these tough conditions, a few hardy plants and animals still manage to survive. You might spot some small rodents and a few bird species that have adapted to the extreme conditions.

Finally, if you keep going, you'll reach the arctic zone at the very top of Kilimanjaro. Here, it's freezing cold, with snow and glaciers covering the ground. Glaciers are giant sheets of ice, and even though Kilimanjaro is near the equator—a region typically known for warm weather—its high altitude means it can still support ice and snow at the summit. However, these glaciers are slowly melting due to climate change, and scientists worry they might disappear entirely in a few decades. Standing on Uhuru Peak, you would see an amazing view of Africa from the top of this icy, snowy world, with clouds floating below you and the vast landscape stretching out as far as the eye can see.

Climbing Kilimanjaro is no easy task. It takes days to reach the top, and climbers need to prepare well for the journey. As they ascend, the air becomes thinner, making it harder to breathe. Some people experience altitude sickness, which can cause headaches, nausea, and fatigue because their bodies aren't used to the lower oxygen levels. Experienced guides help climbers pace themselves to adjust to the altitude. They encourage people to climb "pole pole," which means "slowly" in Swahili. Taking it slow helps climbers adapt to the conditions and makes the journey safer.

Kilimanjaro is also a place of cultural importance. For centuries, local communities have lived near the mountain, and they have their own stories and legends about it. The Chagga people, who are one of the ethnic groups in the area, have deep-rooted beliefs about Kilimanjaro and consider it a sacred place. Some legends describe it as a home for gods, while others tell stories of spirits that watch over the mountain and its forests. Climbers often respect these beliefs, seeing Kilimanjaro as not only a physical challenge but also a place of mystery and beauty.

Each year, thousands of climbers from different countries arrive to test themselves against the Mighty Peak of Africa. Some want to experience the adventure, while others come to achieve a personal goal, like reaching the highest point on the continent. Even though the journey can be tough, many climbers say the view from Uhuru Peak, standing above the clouds and seeing Africa spread out below, is an unforgettable experience that makes every step worth it.

Mount Kilimanjaro's nickname, "The Roof of Africa," truly fits because of its towering height and impressive beauty. It's more than just a mountain—it's a symbol of natural wonder, cultural richness, and the spirit of exploration. The Mighty Peak of Africa continues to inspire people from all walks of life, drawing them to Tanzania to witness its magic, climb its slopes, and leave with memories of one of Earth's most extraordinary places.

Chapter 2: How Mount Kilimanjaro Was Formed

Mount Kilimanjaro's formation is a fascinating story that takes us back millions of years to a time when the Earth's surface was very different from today. The mountain formed as a result of volcanic activity caused by powerful forces deep inside the Earth. It all began with the movements of giant plates, called tectonic plates, which make up the Earth's outer layer. These plates are always moving, even if we can't feel it, and sometimes they shift in ways that create huge cracks or rifts in the Earth's crust. In East Africa, the movement of these tectonic plates created what we now call the East African Rift System. This massive rift stretches across several countries, splitting the land apart and making way for volcanic eruptions. Mount Kilimanjaro sits right on this rift, which played a big role in its creation.

Millions of years ago, when the tectonic plates began to move, magma—hot, melted rock from deep within the Earth—started to rise up through these cracks. As the magma reached the surface, it erupted in violent explosions, and with each eruption, layers of lava piled up, eventually forming a mountain. This is how most volcanoes grow, little by little, with each eruption adding more material to the mountain. Kilimanjaro was no different. It took thousands of eruptions over millions of years to create the massive mountain we see today.

What makes Mount Kilimanjaro unique is that it wasn't formed by just one volcanic eruption. In fact, three separate volcanoes erupted to create the mountain's different peaks. These three volcanic cones are named Shira, Mawenzi, and Kibo. Shira was the first volcano to erupt, and it began forming around 2.5 million years ago. Over time, Shira's eruptions built a large mountain, but eventually, it stopped erupting and became what scientists call an extinct volcano, which means it will never erupt again. Shira's peak has eroded over time, so now it's a flat plateau, or wide, open area, rather than a tall cone like the others.

After Shira's eruptions stopped, the second volcano, Mawenzi, began to form. Mawenzi erupted many times, and it created a rugged, steep peak with sharp ridges and deep valleys. Mawenzi's cone looks very jagged compared to the smoother slopes of Shira. Like Shira, Mawenzi eventually stopped erupting, and it also became an extinct volcano. Although it no longer has volcanic activity, Mawenzi's shape is still impressive and adds to Kilimanjaro's unique appearance.

The third and tallest cone, Kibo, is the most recent to form and is the peak that gives Kilimanjaro its great height. Kibo began erupting around 460,000 years ago, much later than Shira and Mawenzi, and it grew taller with each eruption until it became the highest point in Africa. Kibo is also unique because, unlike Shira and Mawenzi, it is not extinct; it's considered a dormant volcano. This means Kibo could still erupt someday, even though it's been thousands of years since the last eruption. The last major activity on Kibo happened around 200,000 years ago, and since then, it has been quiet. But scientists keep a close eye on it just in case it ever shows signs of waking up again.

As Kibo erupted over thousands of years, layers of lava and ash built up, creating the smooth, rounded peak we see today, called Uhuru Peak. The eruptions also helped form glaciers and ice fields on the mountain, especially near the summit. Although Kilimanjaro is located close to the equator, where it's usually warm, the high altitude of Kibo allows ice to form and stay year-round. However, these glaciers are slowly melting due to climate change, which worries scientists, as the glaciers are a beautiful and unique part of Kilimanjaro's landscape.

During the formation of Kilimanjaro, other natural forces were at work as well. Over millions of years, wind and rain wore down some of the mountain's rock, shaping its slopes and peaks. Erosion, which is the process of rocks breaking down and being carried away by wind and water, helped form Kilimanjaro's unique landscape. Shira, for example, once had a higher peak, but erosion wore it down into the flat plateau we see today. Mawenzi's sharp ridges were also partly shaped by erosion, which made it rough and rugged compared to the smoother Kibo.

Kilimanjaro's volcanic cones, each with its own story, combine to create a mountain like no other in the world. With Shira's ancient plateau, Mawenzi's steep and rocky ridges, and Kibo's icy summit, Kilimanjaro has an incredibly diverse and unique landscape. Each part of the mountain reflects different stages of volcanic activity over millions of years.

The mountain's creation didn't just stop once the volcanoes cooled down. Earthquakes and smaller tremors still happen in the East African Rift region because the tectonic plates are always moving. These small movements help remind us that Kilimanjaro's story is still connected to the powerful forces deep within the Earth. Even though it no longer erupts, Kilimanjaro remains a symbol of the power and beauty of nature. Scientists continue to study the mountain to understand how volcanic mountains like it are formed, and climbers from all over the world come to admire its breathtaking beauty, shaped by millions of years of Earth's natural processes.

Chapter 3: The Great Glaciers on Top

The glaciers on top of Mount Kilimanjaro are like a magical frozen world high above the warm plains of Africa. These "great glaciers" are massive sheets of ice and snow that cover parts of Kilimanjaro's summit, making it one of the few places on Earth where you can find such icy formations near the equator. Seeing these glaciers up close is like stepping into another world; they are bright, glistening, and pure, sitting quietly on the mountain's slopes. These glaciers have been part of Kilimanjaro for thousands of years, formed through a natural process involving snowfall, freezing temperatures, and the high altitude of the mountain.

Although Kilimanjaro is located close to the equator, where it is usually hot and humid, its summit is so high—over 19,000 feet—that it reaches a zone where temperatures are extremely cold. This cold air, combined with the occasional snowfall at the peak, allows glaciers to form and survive. Every time it snows on Kilimanjaro, the snow layers pile up and get packed tightly over time, eventually becoming thick ice. This compacted ice is what makes up the glaciers. The air is thin up there, with low oxygen levels, and there's less protection from the sun's rays, which makes it a tough environment for most living things but perfect for these thick sheets of ice.

There are a few major glaciers on Kilimanjaro, each with its own shape and location. The largest and most famous is the Furtwängler Glacier, which sits near Uhuru Peak, the highest point on the mountain. This glacier is named after Walter Furtwängler, one of the first people to successfully reach Kilimanjaro's summit in 1912. The Furtwängler Glacier is like a giant ice cap, covering a portion of the summit with bright white ice that glows in the sunlight. Nearby, there are other smaller glaciers, each adding to the icy landscape at the top of the mountain.

Kilimanjaro's glaciers look breathtaking, but they are also fragile. Because of their position so high on the mountain, they are affected by changes in climate and temperature. In the early 1900s, Kilimanjaro's glaciers were much larger than they are today, covering a vast area of the summit. Back then, they spread far across the top, blanketing more of the mountain in thick ice. However, over the years, scientists noticed that the glaciers began to shrink. This process, called "glacier retreat," means that the glaciers are slowly melting and losing size. Each year, a little more ice disappears, and some scientists believe that the glaciers may eventually vanish altogether.

The reason the glaciers are melting has a lot to do with climate change. As temperatures on Earth gradually rise, the ice at Kilimanjaro's peak melts faster than it can be replaced by new snowfall. Even though it still snows on the mountain, it isn't enough to keep the glaciers growing. Instead, the warm air, intense sunlight, and dry conditions cause the ice to melt bit by bit. The glaciers are also impacted by the lack of humidity on Kilimanjaro; with drier air, there is less moisture available to help create new snow and ice.

People who climb Kilimanjaro and reach the summit often say that seeing the glaciers up close is one of the most unforgettable sights. The ice sparkles under the sunlight, and climbers can see deep blue crevices and cracks within the glaciers, which show how thick and solid the ice is. In some places, the ice is several meters thick, creating small walls and ridges that seem almost like frozen waves frozen in time. These crevices, along with the icy formations, give the glaciers a magical, otherworldly appearance. It's almost like being at the North or South Pole, even though climbers are standing right above the African savannas and rainforests below.

In addition to being beautiful, Kilimanjaro's glaciers are important for understanding Earth's climate. Scientists study the glaciers to learn more about how the planet's temperatures and weather patterns have changed over time. Ice from glaciers can contain tiny bubbles of air trapped thousands of years ago, which gives scientists clues about what the Earth's atmosphere was like long before people were around. By analyzing these bubbles, scientists can learn more about how temperatures, greenhouse gases, and other factors have changed over thousands of years. Kilimanjaro's glaciers are like nature's time capsules, holding secrets of the Earth's past.

One of the most fascinating things about these glaciers is how they've survived for so long in such an unexpected place. The glaciers on Kilimanjaro are among the only tropical glaciers in the world, along with a few others found in places like the Andes Mountains in South America and some peaks in Indonesia. This makes Kilimanjaro very special, as there are few places where you can see glaciers so close to the equator. But the glaciers' unusual location also makes them more vulnerable to climate change because they are in an area where temperatures are generally warmer.

Some scientists predict that if the glaciers continue to melt at the same rate, they may disappear completely in the coming decades. This would be a huge loss for the mountain's ecosystem, as well as for the cultural and scientific significance of Kilimanjaro. Many people feel sad at the thought of Kilimanjaro losing its glaciers, as they are a key part of the mountain's identity and beauty. Local communities who live near Kilimanjaro, as well as visitors from around the world, hope that efforts to combat climate change will help preserve what's left of these ancient glaciers.

Kilimanjaro's glaciers have witnessed countless sunsets, storms, and starlit nights over thousands of years. They are a symbol of endurance and beauty, surviving high up on the mountain through both harsh conditions and warm climates. Even though they're slowly shrinking, their legacy continues, reminding people of the beauty and fragility of nature. The great glaciers on top of Kilimanjaro are more than just ice; they are a natural wonder, a glimpse into the past, and a precious part of one of Africa's most iconic landscapes.

Chapter 4: Unique Animals of the Mountain

The animals on Mount Kilimanjaro are as fascinating as the mountain itself, and many of them are unique to this high-altitude environment. Kilimanjaro, with its diverse climate zones, is like a natural playground for a variety of animals that are perfectly suited to the conditions at each level of the mountain. From lush rainforests filled with lively monkeys to high alpine deserts where only the toughest creatures survive, Kilimanjaro's wildlife is a blend of common African animals and some rare species that are harder to find anywhere else. Each zone has its own set of animals, and as you go higher up, the animals get fewer but even more unique, adapting to the cold and sparse environment.

At the base of Kilimanjaro, you'll find animals that are commonly seen in African grasslands and savannas, like elephants, buffaloes, and antelopes. These large animals graze on the open grasslands surrounding the mountain and are often seen near the forests that cover Kilimanjaro's lower slopes. Elephants, especially, are a magnificent sight to see as they move through the forests, looking for food and water. They leave behind big footprints and trails, which other animals use to find water sources or navigate the dense vegetation. Sometimes, buffaloes are also seen here, moving in herds. They are powerful animals that help shape the landscape as they eat grass, clear paths, and provide food for the big predators that roam nearby.

As you move up into the rainforest zone, you start to encounter a whole new variety of animals, especially primates, like the playful blue monkeys and the black-and-white colobus monkeys. Blue monkeys are known for their social behavior and are often seen swinging through the trees in groups, calling to each other with chattering sounds. They're not actually blue, but their fur has a slight bluish tint in certain light, which is how they got their name. Blue monkeys spend a lot of time in the treetops, eating fruits, leaves, and insects. The black-and-white colobus monkeys, on the other hand, are some of the most beautiful monkeys on the mountain, with long, fluffy tails and striking black-and-white fur. They move gracefully through the trees, leaping from branch to branch with ease. Unlike the blue monkeys, colobus monkeys don't have thumbs, which makes their leaping skills even more impressive!

In addition to monkeys, the rainforest zone is home to several bird species. One of the most colorful birds found here is the Hartlaub's turaco, a vibrant green bird with a bright red crest and wings. When it flies, you can see flashes of red and green, making it easy to spot against the green leaves. There are also sunbirds, small birds with iridescent feathers that shimmer in the sunlight. Sunbirds have long, curved beaks and feed on nectar from flowers, much like hummingbirds. They play an important role in pollinating the plants on the mountain, helping the flowers and trees reproduce. The rainforest is full of other birds, too, from large hornbills with their unique bills to small, swift birds that dart through the trees, creating a symphony of sounds.

Moving higher up into the heath and moorland zone, the landscape starts to change, and so do the animals. In this area, you'll find creatures that are adapted to both the open spaces and cooler temperatures. One interesting animal here is the Kilimanjaro tree hyrax, a small, furry creature that looks a bit like a large guinea pig. Despite its small size, the tree hyrax is actually closely related to elephants! They live in rocky areas and feed on plants. Tree hyraxes are mostly nocturnal, meaning they're active at night, and they have loud calls that echo through the moorland, especially at dusk and dawn. These calls are one way they communicate with other hyraxes and mark their territory.

The moorland zone is also home to some unique birds, like the scarlet-tufted malachite sunbird. This bird has bright green feathers with long, colorful tail feathers that make it look striking as it perches on the plants. The scarlet-tufted malachite sunbird feeds on nectar from the giant lobelias and other plants that grow in this part of Kilimanjaro. These plants have adapted to the cooler climate, and so have the sunbirds that rely on them. Other small animals, like lizards and insects, also live in this zone, finding shelter among the rocks and plants.

As you reach the alpine desert zone, the animals become even more scarce. This part of the mountain is much colder, with very little vegetation, so only the hardiest animals can survive here. One of the animals you might find is the Mount Kilimanjaro mole-rat. This small, burrowing rodent lives underground to escape the cold and searches for food by digging through the soil. Mole-rats are incredibly tough and can survive on very little food. They mostly eat roots and tubers, which they find by digging through the rocky ground. By living underground, mole-rats stay warm and protect themselves from predators and the cold air above.

One of the rarest animals seen near the summit is the Kilimanjaro leopard. Leopards are solitary and elusive animals, and they are rarely seen on Kilimanjaro. However, there is a famous story about a frozen leopard carcass that was discovered near the summit of the mountain many years ago. No one knows how the leopard ended up so high on Kilimanjaro, but it shows just how far these big cats can roam. The presence of the leopard remains a mystery, but it has added to Kilimanjaro's legend and mystery, making it an even more fascinating mountain.

Above the alpine desert is the summit zone, where the air is so thin and cold that very few animals can survive. This part of Kilimanjaro is mostly barren, with only rocks, ice, and snow. Because of the extreme conditions, no animals permanently live here, but occasionally, birds like ravens are seen flying near the summit. Ravens are incredibly adaptable birds and can survive in a variety of environments. They may come to the summit zone in search of food or simply because they are curious and able to withstand the harsh conditions for short periods. Ravens are smart and resourceful, often scavenging for food, and they are known to follow climbers, hoping to pick up scraps or leftovers.

The animals of Kilimanjaro are not only remarkable for their diversity but also for their adaptability to such a range of climates. From the warm, lush rainforests at the base to the cold, desolate summit, each animal on Kilimanjaro has found a way to survive in its specific zone. They contribute to the mountain's unique ecosystem, playing roles in pollination, seed dispersal, and maintaining the balance of nature. The wildlife here is a reminder of how interconnected life is, with each species contributing to the ecosystem in its own way.

For those who climb Kilimanjaro, encountering these animals adds an extra layer of adventure. The sight of a curious monkey in the forest, the sound of a hyrax calling at dawn, or the flash of a sunbird's colorful feathers creates memories that last a lifetime. Kilimanjaro's unique animals are a big part of what makes this mountain so special.

Chapter 5: Plants and Forests of Kilimanjaro

The plants and forests of Mount Kilimanjaro are just as impressive as the mountain itself, creating a green wonderland that changes as you climb higher. Because Kilimanjaro has such a range of climates, from warm and humid to freezing cold, it's home to many different kinds of plants, each adapted to their unique environment. From the lush rainforests at the base to the hardy shrubs and mosses near the summit, Kilimanjaro's plant life shows the incredible adaptability of nature. As you move up the mountain, you can see plants gradually changing, becoming smaller and tougher to survive in harsher conditions.

At the lower slopes of the mountain, you'll find fertile farmland where local people grow crops like bananas, coffee, and maize. This area benefits from rich volcanic soil, which makes it ideal for agriculture. Coffee farms, in particular, are common here, as the soil and climate provide the perfect conditions for coffee plants to thrive. Coffee from Kilimanjaro is famous around the world for its rich, smooth flavor, and it's one of the important crops for the people who live near the mountain. The farms also have small patches of forest and scattered trees, which provide shade and help preserve the soil. The farms are alive with color, with bright green banana trees, the darker green of coffee plants, and splashes of color from local flowers.

Above the farmland, the mountain is covered in dense rainforest, one of the most vibrant and lively parts of Kilimanjaro. The rainforest zone is warm, moist, and filled with tall trees that create a thick, leafy canopy. This canopy forms a green ceiling that blocks most of the sunlight, keeping the forest floor cool and shady. The trees here are tall and mighty, reaching up to 100 feet in height, and their trunks are often covered with moss, ferns, and other small plants that cling to them. One of the most striking trees in this forest is the African olive tree, which has strong branches and provides food and shelter for many animals.

The rainforest is also filled with flowers and plants that add bright colors to the green surroundings. Orchids, which are known for their beautiful and delicate flowers, grow on some of the trees, their blossoms peeking out from the greenery. These orchids are epiphytes, meaning they grow on the surface of other plants and trees instead of in the soil. They attach themselves to tree branches and absorb water from the air, thriving in the moist rainforest climate. Their flowers are tiny and intricate, with colors ranging from white and yellow to purple, adding beauty to the forest canopy.

The forest floor in the rainforest zone is a soft, moist layer covered in fallen leaves, plants, and small shrubs. You'll find ferns with delicate fronds, as well as wildflowers and vines that twist and turn, reaching toward the light. One plant that stands out is the giant nettle, which can grow up to 10 feet tall! Despite its stinging leaves, it provides shelter for many insects, and animals sometimes use it as cover. Mosses and lichens, which thrive in the damp conditions, cover rocks and tree trunks, creating a lush carpet that makes the forest feel ancient and mysterious.

As you continue climbing, the rainforest starts to give way to the heath and moorland zone. In this zone, the plants are shorter, and the trees are fewer. The landscape changes into open, grassy areas filled with shrubs, grasses, and hardy plants that can withstand the cooler temperatures and stronger winds. One of the most iconic plants here is the giant heather, a tall, tree-like shrub that can grow up to 30 feet high. Unlike the heather plants found in cooler parts of the world, Kilimanjaro's giant heather has adapted to grow in large, tree-like shapes, creating small clusters of shade where animals can rest.

Another remarkable plant in the heath and moorland zone is the giant lobelia. This plant looks a bit like a giant pineapple, with thick, spiky leaves that can grow over 6 feet tall. The giant lobelia has adapted to the cold by developing a special way to protect itself. At night, it closes its leaves to trap warm air, keeping the inside of the plant a little warmer than the chilly air outside. In the morning, it opens up again, releasing any frost that may have formed. This adaptation helps the lobelia survive the freezing temperatures that sometimes occur in the moorland zone, even though it's still close to the equator.

As you move further up into the alpine desert zone, the plants become even more unusual. The alpine desert is cold, dry, and has very little water, making it hard for plants to survive here. The plants in this zone have to be tough and resilient, able to withstand strong winds, freezing nights, and intense sunlight during the day. You'll find small, low-growing plants that hug the ground, like mosses and lichens. These plants grow slowly, but they are incredibly hardy, able to survive in some of the harshest conditions on Earth. Because of the lack of water, these plants are small and close to the ground, reducing their exposure to the drying wind and conserving any moisture they can find.

One of the plants in the alpine desert that stands out is the everlasting flower. This flower grows close to the ground and has tiny, papery petals that help it retain moisture in the dry, windy environment. The petals are often a silvery or pale yellow color, which reflects sunlight, keeping the flower cool and preventing it from drying out. The everlasting flower is called "everlasting" because it can retain its shape and color for a long time, even after it's picked. It's a symbol of resilience on Kilimanjaro, as it manages to thrive in a place where very few plants can survive.

Near the summit, in the arctic zone, the environment becomes so extreme that only a few hardy mosses and lichens are able to survive. The arctic zone is covered in rocks, ice, and snow, with almost no soil or water for plants to grow. This zone is incredibly cold, with temperatures dropping well below freezing, and there is little oxygen in the air. The few plants that do survive here are specially adapted to withstand the cold, growing in small, sheltered cracks in the rocks where they can find some protection from the freezing winds. These plants are among the toughest in the world, able to survive where almost nothing else can.

The different plant zones on Kilimanjaro are like a journey through many different ecosystems, each with its own unique species and adaptations. From the green, lively rainforests to the sparse, rocky summit, the plants of Kilimanjaro are a testament to the power of nature to adapt to every type of environment. They play a crucial role in supporting the animals and insects that live on the mountain, providing food, shelter, and oxygen. Even though Kilimanjaro's plants may seem less famous than its glaciers or animals, they are essential to the mountain's ecosystem, helping to sustain life in this extraordinary landscape.

Chapter 6: The People Who Live Near the Mountain

The people who live near Mount Kilimanjaro have a unique connection to the mountain that goes back for generations. They see Kilimanjaro as not just a towering peak, but as a guardian, a source of life, and a symbol of pride. These communities live in the villages and small towns surrounding the mountain, and they include several different groups, each with its own culture, language, and history. Some of the main groups are the Chagga, the Maasai, and the Pare people, who all have fascinating stories about their relationship with the mountain. For them, Kilimanjaro is much more than just a natural wonder; it's a place full of spiritual meaning and practical importance.

The Chagga people are the largest group living near Kilimanjaro, and their villages are mostly found on the mountain's fertile lower slopes. They are known for their farming skills, which have allowed them to make a good living on the mountain's rich volcanic soil. The Chagga plant coffee, bananas, and maize, along with other crops, which they sell in local markets or use to support their families. The coffee grown by the Chagga is especially famous and has a rich, delicious flavor that's popular around the world. Coffee is more than just a crop for the Chagga—it's a part of their culture and history. Many Chagga families have small coffee farms, and the crop has helped them prosper and maintain a strong community.

In Chagga villages, you'll see banana trees everywhere, creating a green landscape with patches of dark coffee plants growing under their shade. The banana plants have wide leaves that protect the coffee plants from the strong sun, helping them grow better. These bananas aren't just for eating—the Chagga people also use them to make a local drink called *mbege*, a traditional banana beer that's often shared during community gatherings and celebrations. Making *mbege* is a skill passed down from generation to generation, and it's considered a symbol of friendship and hospitality. When there's a wedding, a festival, or even just a get-together, the Chagga come together to share *mbege*, talk, and celebrate.

One of the unique things about the Chagga people is their irrigation system, which is centuries old and still works well today. Long ago, the Chagga built canals to carry water from Kilimanjaro's streams down to their farms, even during dry seasons. This system, known as the *utawa* system, is a marvel of engineering, especially considering it was built without modern tools. The *utawa* system allows water to reach the crops even on steep hillsides, which has made it possible for the Chagga to grow more food and support larger families. The canals are carefully maintained by the community, and each person knows their role in keeping the water flowing. This system has helped the Chagga thrive for many generations, allowing them to live in harmony with Kilimanjaro.

The Chagga people also have strong beliefs and legends about Kilimanjaro. In Chagga folklore, the mountain is considered a sacred place, and many believe it is home to spirits or gods. They tell stories about the mountain's mysterious power and beauty, and these stories are passed down through generations. Some legends say that the mountain has treasures hidden within it, while others warn of dangers or protectors who guard Kilimanjaro. These tales show the deep respect the Chagga have for the mountain and how they see it as a place that holds mysteries beyond human understanding.

Another group living near Kilimanjaro is the Maasai, who are famous for their distinct culture, colorful clothing, and semi-nomadic lifestyle. Unlike the Chagga, the Maasai are traditionally herders, and they rely on cattle for their way of life. The Maasai believe that all cattle on Earth were given to them by their god, Enkai, and cattle are an essential part of their identity and culture. They use cattle for milk, meat, and hides, and they measure wealth in terms of how many cattle they own. The Maasai are tall, proud people who wear bright red and blue shukas, or wraps, which make them stand out in the landscape. They are skilled in protecting their herds and can often be seen with their cattle in the grasslands that surround Kilimanjaro.

While the Maasai don't live directly on the mountain, they often bring their cattle to graze on Kilimanjaro's lower slopes during certain times of the year. The Maasai believe that Kilimanjaro is a sacred place and that the mountain's streams and plants have healing powers. Some Maasai go to the mountain's forests to collect medicinal plants, which they use to treat illnesses and injuries. They have a vast knowledge of the local plants and know which ones can heal wounds, reduce pain, or help with fevers. This knowledge has been passed down over centuries, and it shows the Maasai's deep understanding of their natural surroundings.

The Maasai are known for their incredible jumping dance, known as the *adumu*, which is often performed during celebrations or ceremonies. The young warriors, or *morans*, jump high in the air while chanting and clapping, showing their strength and endurance. The *adumu* is not just a dance but a way for Maasai warriors to demonstrate their bravery and skill. When visitors come to Kilimanjaro, the Maasai sometimes perform their dance as a way to share their culture and welcome others to their land. The Maasai also make and sell beaded jewelry, including necklaces, bracelets, and earrings, which are decorated with colorful patterns and symbols. These crafts have become popular souvenirs for visitors to Kilimanjaro, helping to support the Maasai community.

The Pare people are another group who live close to Mount Kilimanjaro, mainly to the southeast of the mountain. The Pare are known for their skills in farming, especially in growing crops like cassava, yams, and millet. They are also known for their craftsmanship, creating pottery, baskets, and tools that are used in everyday life. The Pare have a strong tradition of environmental conservation and are careful to protect their land and resources. They practice sustainable farming methods to ensure that the soil remains fertile and that future generations can continue to live off the land.

For the people around Kilimanjaro, the mountain is not just a geographical feature; it's a source of livelihood and a spiritual symbol. Many of them make a living from the tourism that the mountain brings, working as guides, porters, or cooks for the climbers who come from around the world to reach Kilimanjaro's summit. Local people help climbers by carrying heavy gear, cooking meals, and guiding them through the mountain's various routes. These jobs provide a vital income for families and have helped the surrounding communities to thrive. Tourists often learn about the local culture through their interactions with the guides and porters, who share stories about the mountain's history, the plants and animals, and the daily lives of the people who live near Kilimanjaro.

Porters are especially important for climbers, as they carry much of the heavy equipment needed for the journey up the mountain. These porters are known for their incredible strength and stamina, as they manage to carry large loads up steep paths, often at high altitudes. They play a crucial role in helping climbers reach the summit safely and comfortably. The guides and porters know the mountain well, including its unpredictable weather and challenging terrain, and their knowledge helps climbers succeed in their journey. For many local people, working as a guide or porter is not just a job but a way to share their love and respect for Kilimanjaro with others.

Kilimanjaro has also influenced the beliefs, stories, and art of the people living nearby. Artists often create paintings, carvings, or sculptures that show the mountain, its animals, and its people. These pieces of art reflect the pride and connection that local people feel towards Kilimanjaro. They see the mountain as a part of their heritage, something to be respected and preserved. Many of them hope that

Kilimanjaro's forests, glaciers, and unique wildlife will be protected for future generations to enjoy and learn from.

For the Chagga, the Maasai, the Pare, and other nearby communities, Mount Kilimanjaro is more than just a mountain. It's a symbol of resilience, unity, and tradition. It shapes their daily lives and inspires their stories, art, and beliefs. They respect Kilimanjaro's power and beauty, and in return, the mountain provides them with food, water, jobs, and cultural pride.

Chapter 7: Early Explorers and Adventurers

Early explorers and adventurers who set their sights on Mount Kilimanjaro were among the most daring and determined people of their time. These brave individuals came from faraway lands to see the legendary mountain, hoping to uncover its mysteries and reach its icy peak. Back then, Kilimanjaro was shrouded in mystery, and few knew what lay at its top. Stories of a massive mountain with snow at its summit, right near the hot equator, were hard to believe for many people. But as explorers heard these tales, their curiosity grew, sparking a desire to see Kilimanjaro for themselves and conquer its challenging heights.

One of the first recorded sightings of Mount Kilimanjaro by Europeans was in the early 19th century, when German missionaries and explorers began to travel into East Africa. A German missionary named Johann Rebmann, who had traveled to Tanzania, was one of the first Europeans to document seeing the snow-capped peak of Kilimanjaro in 1848. Rebmann was fascinated by what he saw, but when he told others back home, they didn't believe him. How could there be snow in Africa, especially on a mountain so close to the equator? Rebmann's report was met with disbelief, and many scientists in Europe dismissed it as impossible. They thought he must have made a mistake, or perhaps he had seen white clouds that only looked like snow from a distance. Despite their doubts, Rebmann's report sparked interest, and soon other explorers began to wonder if there was indeed a towering mountain in East Africa with snow on top.

After Rebmann, another German missionary named Johannes Krapf also saw Kilimanjaro and reported his sighting. Like Rebmann, Krapf faced disbelief, but his report further convinced some people that perhaps these missionaries were telling the truth. Krapf's and

Rebmann's accounts were published in Europe, and slowly, more explorers began to consider visiting Kilimanjaro to see it for themselves. These reports helped to put Kilimanjaro on the map, so to speak, drawing the attention of adventurous souls who wanted to solve the mystery of the mountain's snow-capped peak.

One of the most famous explorers of Kilimanjaro was a German geographer and cartographer named Hans Meyer. Meyer was determined to reach the summit and be the first person to stand on Kilimanjaro's highest peak. In the late 1880s, he made his first attempt, but he faced enormous challenges. Kilimanjaro's slopes were steep and covered in thick forests, and as he climbed higher, he encountered unpredictable weather, freezing temperatures, and strong winds. The altitude made it difficult to breathe, and Meyer and his team struggled to adapt to the thin air. Meyer's first attempt to climb Kilimanjaro ended in failure, but he was determined to try again.

In 1889, Hans Meyer returned to Kilimanjaro with a new plan and a stronger team. This time, he was accompanied by a local guide named Yohani Kinyala Lauwo, who was a Chagga tribesman familiar with the mountain's lower slopes. Together, they faced many obstacles, including rough terrain and freezing temperatures, but their combined knowledge and teamwork helped them reach new heights. As they climbed higher, the air became thin, and each step became harder than the last. Meyer and Lauwo persevered, finally reaching the summit of Kilimanjaro's Kibo peak on October 6, 1889. Meyer was overjoyed and recorded his achievement, noting the spectacular view of the mountain's glaciers and the clouds stretching far below. This marked the first recorded successful ascent of Kilimanjaro, and Meyer became famous for his daring accomplishment. The journey had been incredibly difficult, but Meyer's success inspired others to believe that the summit of Kilimanjaro could be reached.

Hans Meyer's story encouraged other adventurers to try their luck on Kilimanjaro, and soon more explorers made the journey. They were curious about the strange plants and animals they saw along the way, and many brought back samples to show scientists back in Europe. They documented Kilimanjaro's unique landscapes, from the lush rainforests to the barren alpine desert and the icy glaciers at the top. Explorers marveled at how quickly the environment changed as they climbed, with each zone bringing new discoveries. These early expeditions taught the world a great deal about Kilimanjaro's natural wonders and its diverse ecosystems.

During this time, some explorers were also interested in Kilimanjaro for scientific reasons. They wanted to study its climate, geology, and glaciers to understand how such a tall mountain could exist in the middle of a hot tropical region. Scientists and geographers tried to figure out why Kilimanjaro had snow on top despite being so close to the equator. They studied the mountain's glaciers, the way plants changed with altitude, and the effects of altitude on the human body. Their studies led to new knowledge about high-altitude environments and the adaptations needed to survive in such conditions.

As the years passed, Kilimanjaro continued to attract explorers, scientists, and adventurers. Some came to map its terrain, while others were drawn by the thrill of climbing its rugged slopes. Every climber faced challenges, including extreme cold, lack of oxygen, and unpredictable weather, but they also experienced the beauty and majesty of Kilimanjaro up close. Their stories and discoveries helped to spread the fame of Kilimanjaro even further, and soon people from all around the world dreamed of visiting this unique mountain.

Throughout the 20th century, more climbers made their way to Kilimanjaro. As equipment and clothing improved, it became easier for people to attempt the climb, although it remained a challenging adventure. Some climbers came for scientific research, studying the effects of climate change on the mountain's glaciers, which were beginning to shrink. Others came for the sheer thrill of reaching the summit and standing on Africa's highest point. Today, climbers from all over the world follow in the footsteps of those early explorers, testing their strength and endurance against Kilimanjaro's demanding slopes.

Even though modern climbers have better gear and more knowledge about the mountain, the spirit of those early explorers lives on in every person who attempts the climb. They still face the same rugged paths, the same thinning air, and the same cold nights that challenged Hans Meyer and his team. The mountain remains as awe-inspiring and challenging as ever, reminding climbers of the courage and determination it took to be among the first to reach its summit.

The early explorers and adventurers who first came to Kilimanjaro helped to reveal its beauty and mystery to the world. Their bravery and perseverance paved the way for future climbers, scientists, and tourists, all eager to experience Kilimanjaro's wonders for themselves. Thanks to their efforts, Kilimanjaro is now one of the most famous mountains in the world, drawing thousands of visitors each year who come to witness its breathtaking landscapes and test themselves on its slopes. The legacy of those early explorers endures, inspiring each new generation to explore, dream, and discover.

Chapter 8: Stories and Legends of Kilimanjaro

Mount Kilimanjaro has fascinated people for centuries, inspiring countless stories and legends. For the people who live near the mountain, it's more than just a towering peak. Kilimanjaro holds a special place in their hearts as a source of mystery, power, and even magic. Generations of local communities, including the Chagga and Maasai, have shared stories about Kilimanjaro that reflect their beliefs, fears, and respect for this mighty mountain. These tales are passed down from parents to children, connecting each new generation to the spirit of Kilimanjaro and the secrets it holds. Some of these legends tell of treasures hidden in the mountain, while others speak of ancient spirits that protect its slopes. Through these stories, Kilimanjaro becomes a living, breathing character in the lives of those who call it their neighbor.

One well-known legend from the Chagga people tells of a powerful spirit or god who lives at the top of Kilimanjaro. According to the legend, this spirit is the guardian of the mountain and watches over the people who live nearby. The spirit is said to protect the mountain's treasures and punish those who try to take them. This belief has been part of Chagga culture for generations, teaching people to respect the mountain and not take more than they need from its forests, water, or land. Some say that if someone climbs too high on Kilimanjaro without proper respect, they may encounter strange weather, get lost, or feel an intense chill, as if the spirit is warning them to turn back. This legend of the mountain's guardian helps to explain the unpredictable nature of Kilimanjaro's weather, where sunny skies can suddenly turn stormy, and temperatures can drop rapidly. For the Chagga, these sudden changes are reminders that Kilimanjaro is powerful and must be respected.

Another Chagga tale tells of a treasure hidden deep within Kilimanjaro, guarded by the mountain's spirit. According to this story, long ago, a Chagga warrior stumbled upon a glittering cave filled with gold and gems while hunting on the mountain's slopes. He tried to take some of the treasure, but as soon as he touched it, a fierce storm swept in, forcing him to flee. When he returned to his village, he shared what he had seen, but no one else could ever find the cave again. It was as if the mountain had hidden it from view to protect its riches. This legend of hidden treasure has captivated people for years, and it adds an air of mystery to Kilimanjaro. Although no one has found this supposed cave of riches, the story continues to be told as a reminder that some things are meant to remain untouched.

The Maasai people, who live on the plains near Kilimanjaro, have their own stories about the mountain. One Maasai legend says that Kilimanjaro was formed during a great battle between two volcanoes—Kilimanjaro and a neighboring mountain named Meru. The story goes that Kilimanjaro and Meru were once great warriors who fought over the land. During their battle, Kilimanjaro's strength proved greater, and he defeated Meru, pushing him farther away. To mark his victory, Kilimanjaro grew taller, reaching toward the sky, while Meru was left smaller and farther to the west. This legend explains why Kilimanjaro stands as the highest peak in Africa, towering over the plains and other mountains. It's a way for the Maasai to tell the story of their land and to show respect for the mighty Kilimanjaro as a symbol of strength and endurance.

There is also a Maasai tale about Kilimanjaro's snowcap, which appears as a white crown on top of the dark mountain. The Maasai say that the snow was placed there by their god, Enkai, to cool the mountain's fiery heart. According to the story, Kilimanjaro was once a volcano that spewed fire and ash, making it dangerous for people to live nearby. Enkai, seeing the harm caused by the volcano, placed a blanket of snow on its peak to calm its fury. Ever since, the snow has kept the mountain peaceful, allowing people to live in its shadow without fear of eruptions. This tale reflects the Maasai's understanding of Kilimanjaro's volcanic nature and their belief that Enkai watches over them and protects their land.

Another fascinating legend from the Chagga people explains the glaciers on Kilimanjaro. The Chagga say that these glaciers are the frozen tears of a great chief who once ruled the land. The chief was deeply saddened by the suffering he saw among his people and the hardship they faced while living near the mountain. He climbed to the top of Kilimanjaro to seek wisdom and guidance. While he was there, he prayed for strength and solutions for his people, and in his sorrow, he wept. His tears, so full of love and concern, turned to ice on the cold mountaintop. They became the glaciers we see today, a reminder of the chief's compassion for his people. The story of the chief's tears serves as a symbol of caring and sacrifice, showing the Chagga people's deep connection to Kilimanjaro and their respect for leaders who look after their community.

Other stories about Kilimanjaro reflect the mountain's role as a place of mystery and challenge. Some people say that the mountain has magical powers and that only those who are pure of heart can reach its summit. This belief adds a sense of wonder and respect for those who attempt to climb Kilimanjaro. According to some legends, climbers who reach the top may experience visions or gain special wisdom. These tales suggest that Kilimanjaro is not just a physical challenge but a spiritual one as well. Climbers are said to feel a sense of awe and humility on the mountain, as if they are connecting with something greater than themselves. The journey to Kilimanjaro's peak is seen as a test of character, courage, and resilience, and those who succeed are considered blessed or transformed.

Some stories also warn of the dangers that lie on Kilimanjaro. There are tales of spirits that guard the mountain, hiding in its forests and caves. The Chagga people believe that these spirits can be protective or mischievous, depending on how climbers treat the mountain. Respecting the mountain, staying humble, and leaving nature undisturbed are seen as ways to avoid angering these spirits. Some climbers have reported strange sounds or feelings of being watched, adding to the eerie mystery of Kilimanjaro. For local people, these stories serve as reminders that Kilimanjaro is a place to be honored and respected. They believe that those who are careless or disrespectful may encounter difficulties on the mountain or be met with bad luck.

In addition to local legends, Kilimanjaro has inspired stories and myths in other parts of the world. When early explorers from Europe heard about Kilimanjaro's snowy peak, they were amazed and began to imagine all sorts of explanations. Some thought the mountain held magical powers or ancient secrets. Writers and adventurers in Europe created stories about Kilimanjaro as a place of mystery, where brave explorers could discover hidden treasures or encounter strange creatures. These tales helped to make Kilimanjaro famous and spread its legend far beyond Africa. Kilimanjaro's unique combination of snow, height, and isolation made it seem like a magical place, capturing the imagination of people around the world.

Over the years, Kilimanjaro has continued to be a source of inspiration for storytellers, climbers, and travelers. Its legends are woven into the fabric of the local culture, reflecting the respect, wonder, and sometimes fear that people feel toward the mountain. For the Chagga, Maasai, and others, these stories connect them to Kilimanjaro, grounding their culture in a deep respect for nature and the powerful forces that shape their lives. The mountain's legends are reminders of Kilimanjaro's strength, beauty, and mystery, and they keep the mountain alive in the minds and hearts of those who live nearby and those who hear its tales from afar.

Today, climbers and tourists who visit Kilimanjaro often learn about these stories, adding to their appreciation of the mountain's rich cultural history. They are told of the powerful spirits, hidden treasures, and heroic ancestors who once climbed its slopes, and they feel a sense of wonder at the idea that Kilimanjaro is not just a physical place but a source of ancient wisdom and spiritual power. These legends add depth to the journey, reminding climbers that they are not just reaching for a mountain peak but touching a piece of history, culture, and mystery.

Chapter 9: Climbing the Mountain: What It Takes

Climbing Mount Kilimanjaro is an adventure that requires courage, preparation, and a love for challenge. At 19,341 feet, it's the highest peak in Africa, which means it's not just any hike—it's an expedition through thick forests, steep paths, and icy altitudes. Climbers from all over the world come to Kilimanjaro to test themselves and experience the thrill of standing on Africa's rooftop, looking out over the clouds. But reaching the summit takes a lot more than just enthusiasm; it takes months of training, careful planning, and a determined mindset.

To begin with, physical fitness is crucial for anyone hoping to climb Kilimanjaro. The mountain has different routes, some more challenging than others, but they all require a lot of energy and stamina. People who want to climb Kilimanjaro often train for months before the climb, building up their strength through exercises like hiking, running, or biking. Walking up a mountain requires strong legs, so climbers focus on exercises that strengthen their muscles, especially their calves and thighs. They also work on their endurance, because the journey to the summit can take up to eight days, with long hours of walking each day. Climbers know that the stronger and more fit they are, the easier it will be to handle Kilimanjaro's tough paths.

Besides physical fitness, climbers need to prepare for the altitude. As you go higher up a mountain, the air gets thinner, meaning there's less oxygen with each breath. This can make it hard to breathe and can lead to a condition called altitude sickness. Altitude sickness happens when the body can't get enough oxygen, and it can cause headaches, dizziness, nausea, and even make you feel very tired. If altitude sickness gets severe, it can even be dangerous, so climbers need to be careful. To get used to the thin air, climbers take their time going up the mountain. This is called "acclimatization," and it helps the body adjust slowly to higher altitudes. Many climbers spend an extra day or two at certain camps along the way to help their bodies adapt. Some even take short hikes to higher points during the day and then come back down to sleep at a lower elevation, which helps their bodies get used to the height.

One of the most important things climbers need to do before the trip is to pack the right gear. Kilimanjaro's climate is unique because it has different weather zones, from warm forests at the base to freezing glaciers at the top. Climbers start their journey in comfortable temperatures, wearing light clothing, but as they go higher, the temperature drops, and they need warmer clothes. Climbers often pack in layers, so they can add or remove clothing as needed. At the summit, it can be extremely cold, with temperatures dropping below freezing, so climbers bring heavy jackets, hats, gloves, and thermal pants to keep warm. The cold, thin air at the top can make even simple tasks feel challenging, so staying warm is essential to keep their energy up and avoid frostbite.

Water and food are also very important on Kilimanjaro. Climbing for hours each day uses up a lot of energy, so climbers need to eat regularly to stay strong. They usually bring high-energy snacks like nuts, dried fruit, and chocolate for quick boosts of energy during the climb. Most people also bring meals that are easy to cook at camp, like pasta, rice, or oatmeal, which provide the carbohydrates they need to keep going. Staying hydrated is equally important because the high altitude can make people dehydrate quickly. Climbers drink several liters of water every day to prevent altitude sickness and keep their bodies working well. They bring water bottles that can hold enough water for a day's hike, and many also bring water purification tablets, as the mountain streams may not always be clean.

Another important part of climbing Kilimanjaro is having a reliable guide. The guides on Kilimanjaro are highly skilled and know the mountain very well. Many of them are from the local Chagga or Maasai communities, and they've spent years climbing its trails. These guides help climbers in many ways. They set a pace that is slow and steady, allowing everyone to adjust to the altitude and prevent exhaustion. They know the safest paths and can spot potential dangers, like loose rocks or sudden weather changes. If someone starts feeling unwell, the guides know what to do and can make sure they get the care they need. Many climbers say that their guides are the real heroes of the journey, providing not only expert guidance but also encouragement and support, helping everyone feel confident as they tackle the mountain.

When climbers finally reach the higher camps, they face the biggest challenge: the summit push. This is usually done at night to reach the peak by sunrise. Climbers wake up around midnight, put on all their warmest clothes, and begin the steepest part of the climb in the dark. Using headlamps to see the rocky path, they slowly make their way upward. The air is very thin at this point, making it hard to breathe, and many climbers have to stop often to catch their breath. The cold can be intense, and the combination of exhaustion, lack of oxygen, and freezing temperatures makes this part of the climb incredibly difficult. But as they get closer to the summit, climbers feel a surge of excitement, knowing they're about to achieve something amazing.

When climbers finally reach the summit, they are greeted by the iconic Uhuru Peak sign, marking the highest point in Africa. Standing at the top of Kilimanjaro, they can see glaciers, snowfields, and a breathtaking view of the land stretching out far below. The feeling of reaching the top after such a hard journey is unforgettable. Climbers take pictures, enjoy the view, and celebrate their accomplishment, knowing they have conquered Africa's highest mountain. For many, this moment is filled with pride, gratitude, and a sense of wonder at the beauty of nature. They know they've achieved something special, something they'll remember for the rest of their lives.

Even though reaching the summit is a huge success, the climb down can also be challenging. After the excitement of reaching the top, climbers still need to be careful as they descend. Going downhill might seem easier, but it can be tough on the knees, and by this time, most people are very tired. The descent takes several hours, and climbers need to stay focused to avoid slipping or tripping on loose rocks. The guides continue to support them, reminding them to drink water and helping them stay motivated. Many climbers say that reaching the base again, knowing they completed the journey safely, brings a sense of relief and accomplishment just as satisfying as reaching the summit.

Climbing Mount Kilimanjaro is not just a physical journey but also an emotional and mental one. It tests every part of a person's strength, determination, and courage. Along the way, climbers experience moments of doubt, exhaustion, and even fear, but they also find new strengths they didn't know they had. The mountain teaches them patience, resilience, and the power of teamwork. It's a journey that brings people closer to nature and closer to themselves. Every step, from the first to the last, is part of an adventure that leaves climbers forever changed. For many, climbing Kilimanjaro is a dream come true, a story they will share for years to come, inspiring others to believe in their own strength and to seek out their own adventures.

Chapter 10: Famous Climbers and Their Journeys

Over the years, Mount Kilimanjaro has drawn climbers from all over the world, each with their own reason for taking on the mighty mountain. Some come to prove their physical strength, others for a once-in-a-lifetime adventure, and some for meaningful causes. Among them are famous climbers whose journeys up Kilimanjaro have made history, inspiring people everywhere. Their stories capture the excitement and challenges of scaling one of the world's most iconic peaks, showing that Kilimanjaro is a place where ordinary people can accomplish extraordinary things.

One of the first explorers to reach the summit of Kilimanjaro was Hans Meyer, a German geologist, and mountaineer. In the late 1800s, Kilimanjaro was an unknown and mysterious peak, rumored to be surrounded by glaciers at the top, even though it stood near the equator. Meyer was curious to see these icy caps with his own eyes. In 1889, after two failed attempts, Meyer finally made it to the top with the help of a skilled local guide named Yohani Kinyala Lauwo. Together, they battled tough terrain, high altitude, and harsh weather. After several days of hiking, they became the first people to officially reach Kilimanjaro's summit, Uhuru Peak. Meyer's journey was groundbreaking and proved that humans could conquer such a high mountain. His adventure made Kilimanjaro famous around the world and inspired others to follow in his footsteps.

Decades later, Anne Lorimor, a grandmother from Arizona, showed that age doesn't have to stop anyone from reaching new heights. At 89, Anne climbed Kilimanjaro to set a world record as the oldest person to reach the summit. Anne's story is remarkable because she didn't start climbing mountains until much later in her life. She didn't let her age or any physical limits hold her back, training hard and keeping a positive attitude throughout her journey. Climbing Kilimanjaro was challenging, but Anne's determination kept her moving forward, step by step. Her goal was to inspire others, especially older people, to believe in themselves and stay active. Her journey up Kilimanjaro proves that it's never too late to chase your dreams.

Another inspiring climber, Kyle Maynard, became the first quadruple amputee to reach the top of Kilimanjaro without any prosthetic limbs. Kyle was born with a condition that left him without arms or legs, but he didn't let that stop him. A motivational speaker, wrestler, and adventurer, Kyle trained hard to prepare for the climb. His journey up Kilimanjaro was incredibly tough, as he had to crawl up the rocky paths using just his hands and feet. His team was there to support him, but Kyle was determined to make it to the top on his own. His climb took ten days, much longer than most people, but he made it all the way to the summit, showing incredible strength and determination. His journey inspired people around the world, showing that no challenge is too great if you have the courage to try.

Another famous climber who made history on Kilimanjaro is Chhurim Sherpa, a mountaineer from Nepal. Chhurim was already known for being the first woman to climb Mount Everest twice in one week, a record that amazed the world. Climbing Kilimanjaro was another achievement in her list of impressive accomplishments. Chhurim's journey was not only about conquering a new mountain but also about showing that women from her homeland, known for their strength and resilience, could take on any challenge. Her adventure on Kilimanjaro inspired many young girls to believe in themselves and to consider mountain climbing as a possibility. Through her climbs, Chhurim became a role model for many, proving that women, too, could stand on top of the world's highest and most challenging peaks.

One climber who took on Kilimanjaro for a cause was Chris Long, a former NFL player. Chris founded an organization called the Waterboys, which works to bring clean water to communities in need.

He decided to climb Kilimanjaro to raise awareness and funds for water projects in Africa. Chris wasn't alone; he brought along several other NFL players, as well as military veterans, to join him on the climb. Together, they called their journey the "Conquering Kili" expedition, and their goal was to inspire others to help with their mission. The team successfully reached the summit, raising enough money to fund clean water projects and provide access to safe drinking water for thousands of people. For Chris and his team, climbing Kilimanjaro was not just an adventure but a way to give back to the communities living near the mountain.

One young climber, Jordan Romero, reached Kilimanjaro's summit as part of his goal to become the youngest person to climb the Seven Summits, the highest peaks on each continent. Jordan was only ten years old when he set out on this challenge, climbing Kilimanjaro with his father and stepmother by his side. Despite his young age, Jordan was determined and well-prepared, training hard to build his endurance and strength. Climbing Kilimanjaro was an important step in his journey, and it showed the world that kids, too, could take on big challenges if they set their minds to it. Jordan's story encourages other young adventurers to believe in themselves and chase their dreams, no matter how big they may seem.

One of the fastest recorded climbs was completed by Karl Egloff, a Swiss-Ecuadorian mountain runner. In 2014, he set a record by climbing up and down Kilimanjaro in just six hours and 42 minutes. This time was incredibly fast, considering that most people take about five to eight days for a round trip. Karl's achievement showed the strength and skill required to move so quickly at high altitudes, where breathing becomes difficult. He trained intensely for the climb, focusing on building his speed and endurance. His record-breaking climb is a testament to the power of dedication and hard work, and it stands as an incredible feat that has inspired mountain runners and climbers around the world.

Famous climbers on Kilimanjaro aren't only those who reach the summit; some climbers bring their unique dreams and challenges to the mountain, making their journeys unforgettable. One such climber, Spencer West, reached the summit even though he had lost both legs at the age of five. Spencer climbed much of the mountain on his hands, using incredible strength and determination. His journey to the top was a fundraiser for clean water projects, and he raised thousands of dollars with every step he took. Spencer's journey was not just a physical challenge but also a way to inspire others to push beyond their limits. He showed the world that physical challenges don't have to hold anyone back from achieving great things.

Finally, the story of Kilian Jornet, a Spanish mountain runner, also stands out. Known for his incredible endurance and speed, Kilian climbed Kilimanjaro in a remarkably fast time, setting a speed record for his ascent. Kilian's love for mountains and adventure shines through in his climbs, and his achievements on Kilimanjaro and other peaks have inspired athletes and climbers everywhere. For Kilian, running and climbing are ways to connect with nature and experience the beauty of mountains up close. His climb on Kilimanjaro demonstrates the unique way that different climbers approach the mountain, some for speed, others for endurance, but all with a deep respect for its majesty.

Each of these famous climbers brought their own goals, skills, and dreams to Kilimanjaro, making the mountain a part of their stories. Their journeys remind us that Kilimanjaro is more than just a tall peak—it's a place where people push themselves, inspire others, and discover new strengths. Whether they climb for personal reasons, to break records, or to help others, these climbers leave a lasting impact on the mountain and all who hear their stories.

Chapter 11: Different Routes Up Kilimanjaro

Mount Kilimanjaro offers several different routes to reach the summit, each with its own unique challenges, scenery, and stories. While every route leads to Uhuru Peak, the highest point on the mountain, they vary in length, difficulty, and the types of landscapes climbers pass through. For anyone who dreams of conquering Kilimanjaro, choosing the right route is an important part of the journey. Some routes are longer and give more time for climbers to adjust to the high altitude, while others are steeper but offer breathtaking views. These routes give climbers options based on their experience, fitness level, and how much they want to see and explore on their way to the top. Let's look at each of the main routes and what makes them special.

One of the most popular routes up Kilimanjaro is the Marangu Route. This route is sometimes called the "Coca-Cola Route" because it's considered one of the easiest and is well-traveled. The Marangu Route is the only path on Kilimanjaro where climbers sleep in huts instead of tents, which some people find more comfortable. The huts provide a simple place to rest, with bunk beds and basic facilities, making it a popular choice for people who want a slightly more comfortable experience. The Marangu Route starts in the lush rainforest zone, with tall trees, colorful birds, and occasional monkeys swinging in the branches. As climbers move higher, they pass through different landscapes, including moorland with wildflowers and giant heather plants. Eventually, they reach the alpine desert zone, where the vegetation becomes sparse, and the ground is rocky and dry. The Marangu Route is a shorter path to the summit, typically taking about five to six days, which means it doesn't give as much time to adjust to the altitude. Because of this, it has a lower success rate for reaching the summit compared to other routes, but it's still a favorite for many climbers.

Another well-loved path is the Machame Route, also known as the "Whiskey Route." This route is more challenging than Marangu, with steeper trails and some sections that require a bit of scrambling over rocks. The Machame Route takes about six to seven days, which gives climbers a better chance to acclimatize to the high altitude. This route is known for its incredible scenery. Starting in the rainforest, climbers gradually make their way up to the moorlands, where they can see giant lobelias and Senecio plants that look almost alien. After this, the route leads through the alpine desert, with wide, open landscapes and rocky paths. One of the highlights of the Machame Route is the Barranco Wall, a steep rock face that climbers have to scale to continue their journey. It might look intimidating at first, but it's safe and manageable with careful steps. This route also offers spectacular views of the glaciers near the summit. Many people choose the Machame Route because of its variety in scenery and because it gives a better chance to adjust to the altitude, making it a favorite for those who want a good balance between challenge and beauty.

The Lemosho Route is another beautiful path up Kilimanjaro, known for its scenic landscapes and quieter trails. The Lemosho Route starts on the western side of the mountain, making it a less crowded option, especially at the beginning. Climbers who take this route begin their journey in the rainforest, where they might spot colobus monkeys and exotic birds. After a couple of days, they move into the heath and moorland zones, where unique plants like the giant groundsels and lobelias grow. The Lemosho Route takes about seven to eight days, which allows climbers plenty of time to acclimatize, giving them a higher chance of reaching the summit. One of the memorable parts of the Lemosho Route is the Shira Plateau, a wide, open area where climbers get their first close-up views of the Kibo peak, Kilimanjaro's main summit. The route also joins up with the Machame Route at the

Shira Plateau, so climbers eventually experience the famous Barranco Wall and other highlights of the Machame path. Many climbers love the Lemosho Route because of its peaceful start, breathtaking views, and excellent chances of reaching the top.

For climbers looking for a unique experience, the Rongai Route is a great choice. This is the only route that starts on the northern side of Kilimanjaro, near the Kenyan border. The Rongai Route offers a different view of the mountain and is often quieter than the southern routes, which some climbers prefer. The route begins in a dry forest area with views of the plains below, giving it a different feel from the rainforest found on other routes. As climbers move higher, they enter the moorlands and then the alpine desert. The Rongai Route is known for being a bit easier than some of the other paths because it has a gentler slope. However, because it's shorter, typically taking six to seven days, it doesn't give as much time for acclimatization, which can make reaching the summit a bit more challenging for some climbers. A unique feature of the Rongai Route is that it offers the chance to see more wildlife, like antelope and elephants, at the lower altitudes. This route is perfect for those looking for a less crowded experience and a different perspective of the mountain.

Another challenging route is the Umbwe Route, known for its steep paths and quick ascent. This route is one of the shortest, taking about five to six days to reach the summit, which means it offers very little time for acclimatization. Because of this, it's considered one of the most difficult routes and is recommended for experienced climbers who are confident in their fitness and ability to handle high altitudes. The Umbwe Route starts with a steep climb through the rainforest, where the trees are thick, and the air is humid. Soon, climbers move into the moorlands and alpine desert, where they're treated to sweeping views of the surrounding valleys and rocky cliffs. The Umbwe Route joins the Machame Route near the Barranco Camp, so climbers on this path also face the Barranco Wall challenge. While the Umbwe Route is tough, it's also incredibly scenic, with dramatic landscapes and a sense of adventure that many experienced climbers love.

The Northern Circuit Route is the longest path on Kilimanjaro, taking about nine days to reach the summit. This route circles around the mountain, offering views from different angles and giving climbers more time to adjust to the altitude. Starting from the west, like the Lemosho Route, the Northern Circuit takes climbers through the rainforest, across the Shira Plateau, and around to the quieter northern slopes. This path is known for its high success rate because it allows plenty of time for acclimatization, making it a great choice for those who want a relaxed pace. The Northern Circuit also gives climbers a chance to see parts of Kilimanjaro that other routes don't, with fewer crowds and unique views. The extra days mean more opportunities to enjoy the changing landscapes, from lush forests to barren deserts and finally to the icy summit. For those who want a complete Kilimanjaro experience, the Northern Circuit offers an in-depth journey with some of the best chances of reaching Uhuru Peak.

Finally, there is the Western Breach Route, which is known for its challenging climb and steep ascent. The Western Breach is the steepest and most technical part of Kilimanjaro, often covered in snow and ice, especially near the summit. Climbers on this route need to be prepared for scrambling and climbing over rocks, and sometimes even snow patches. Because of the difficulty, the Western Breach is recommended only for experienced climbers who are comfortable with steep climbs and colder conditions. The Western Breach Route starts on the Lemosho or Machame paths but then takes a different route up the mountain near the top. While this route is tough, it also offers stunning views and a sense of accomplishment that few other routes can match.

Each route up Kilimanjaro provides a different experience, with unique challenges, landscapes, and views. Whether a climber chooses the shorter, steeper Umbwe Route, the scenic and quiet Rongai Route, or the adventurous Western Breach, every path offers the chance to experience the magic of Kilimanjaro. Climbers get to see how the landscapes change as they move higher, from thick forests filled with wildlife to rocky deserts and icy glaciers at the top. No matter which route they choose, every climber who attempts Kilimanjaro brings back unforgettable memories and a story of their own journey to Africa's highest peak.

Chapter 12: Weather on the Mountain: From Hot to Freezing

Mount Kilimanjaro's weather is truly unique, as it changes dramatically from the bottom to the top. This is because Kilimanjaro is a "sky island," meaning it stands alone, rising high above the flat plains that surround it. Because of its height, Kilimanjaro experiences all sorts of weather patterns as you move up through its various zones. The journey to the summit takes climbers from warm, tropical conditions at the base to freezing, icy conditions at the top. This amazing range of climates makes Kilimanjaro like a mountain of many seasons, and it's one of the reasons the climb is so exciting yet challenging. Let's explore each zone and the weather that comes with it!

At the base of Kilimanjaro, where the journey begins, the weather is warm and humid, much like a tropical rainforest. This zone, called the rainforest zone, gets a lot of rainfall throughout the year, especially from March to May and in November. The temperatures here are mild to warm, usually between 20 and 25 degrees Celsius (68 to 77 degrees Fahrenheit), which feels comfortable. The humidity is high, making the air feel thick and sticky, but it's also what allows the forest to thrive with green trees, vines, and bright flowers. In this rainforest area, clouds often cover the sky, trapping the heat and creating a cozy, lush environment. Rain showers are common, especially in the afternoon, so climbers often start their hike with light rain gear. The rainforest is alive with sounds, from chirping birds to rustling monkeys, and the warm air makes it feel like a tropical paradise. However, climbers know that this warm weather won't last as they move higher up.

As climbers leave the rainforest, they enter the heath and moorland zone, where the weather starts to cool down. This zone is drier than the rainforest, with fewer clouds and less humidity. Temperatures here can range from about 10 to 20 degrees Celsius (50 to 68 degrees

Fahrenheit) during the day, which feels pleasant and refreshing. At night, however, the temperature can drop to freezing, especially at higher points within this zone. Because the moorland zone is more exposed, there are fewer trees, and the wind can be strong, making the air feel even cooler. The plants here are unique and adapted to the cooler, drier conditions. You might see giant lobelias and groundsels that have special ways of surviving in this chilly, windy climate. While the daytime can be sunny and mild, nighttime brings a significant drop in temperature, reminding climbers that they're getting closer to the colder regions of Kilimanjaro.

After the moorland, climbers reach the alpine desert zone, where the weather becomes much harsher. The alpine desert is an area with very little rainfall, and it's much colder than the zones below. During the day, the sun can be intense, and temperatures can reach around 10 to 15 degrees Celsius (50 to 59 degrees Fahrenheit). There are no trees or shade, so climbers feel the full force of the sun's rays, which can make the air feel warmer than it actually is. However, at night, the alpine desert turns freezing, with temperatures often dropping below zero degrees Celsius (32 degrees Fahrenheit). Because there's less air and moisture to trap heat, the warmth from the day escapes quickly after the sun sets. This rapid cooling means that climbers need warm clothing to stay comfortable at night. The alpine desert is a challenging environment with dry, rocky terrain, and the weather can be unpredictable. Winds can pick up, making it feel even colder, and climbers have to be prepared for these sudden changes.

Finally, as climbers approach the summit, they enter the arctic zone, where the weather is extremely cold and challenging. The arctic zone is the highest part of Kilimanjaro and includes the summit, where temperatures can drop as low as -20 degrees Celsius (-4 degrees Fahrenheit) or even lower at night. Here, there is very little oxygen, which makes breathing harder, and the freezing air adds to the difficulty of the climb. During the day, the sun can still shine brightly, but the temperature rarely rises above freezing, so it's cold even in the daylight. Climbers wear layers of warm clothing, including gloves, hats, and heavy jackets, to protect themselves from the biting cold. The arctic zone also has snow and ice, and the glaciers near the summit create a stark, icy landscape. This is a place where only a few specialized plants, like hardy mosses, can survive, and there are no animals or birds. It feels almost like being on another planet, with vast expanses of white snow and ice stretching out around the climbers.

One interesting thing about Kilimanjaro's weather is how quickly it can change. Because the mountain is so tall and isolated, clouds can form suddenly and bring rain, hail, or even snow. Sometimes, climbers start their day in sunshine, only to be caught in a snowstorm as they get closer to the summit. In the lower zones, rain showers are common, especially during the rainy seasons, while in the upper zones, sudden snowfalls can make the climb slippery and cold. Climbers always need to be prepared for these quick changes, carrying waterproof clothing and warm layers to adjust as needed.

The weather on Kilimanjaro is also affected by the time of year. The dry seasons, from December to March and from June to October, are usually the best times to climb because there is less rain, and the skies are often clearer. During the dry season, climbers have a better chance of seeing the stunning views from the summit, as there are fewer clouds to block the view. However, even in the dry season, temperatures at the summit are freezing, and climbers still face cold winds and icy conditions. The rainy seasons, especially from March to May, make the climb more challenging because the paths become muddy and slippery, and visibility can be limited by thick clouds. Despite these challenges, some climbers choose to tackle Kilimanjaro in the rainy season to experience the mountain's lush greenery and the beauty of the rainforest in full bloom.

Kilimanjaro's unique weather zones also mean that climbers can experience a type of "mini world tour" as they move through different climates on their way up. From the warmth of the rainforest to the freezing arctic conditions at the summit, Kilimanjaro provides a rare opportunity to witness the power of nature and the effect of altitude on weather. For climbers, this means carefully preparing for every type of weather, bringing sunscreen for the strong sun, rain gear for the rainforest, and insulated clothing for the icy summit. It's a journey that requires endurance, adaptability, and respect for the mountain's unpredictable weather patterns.

Reaching the summit of Kilimanjaro is like experiencing all four seasons in a single journey, from tropical warmth to winter-like cold. This fascinating range of weather zones makes Kilimanjaro a truly unique mountain and a challenging adventure for anyone who takes on the climb.

Chapter 13: The Amazing Views from the Summit

Reaching the summit of Mount Kilimanjaro is a dream come true for climbers, and one of the most incredible parts of the journey is the breathtaking view from the top. Standing on Kilimanjaro's summit, also known as Uhuru Peak, is like being on top of the world. At 5,895 meters (19,341 feet), it's the highest point in Africa, and the views stretch far and wide across Tanzania and beyond. The sense of achievement and wonder at this height is hard to put into words, but one thing's for sure—seeing the amazing sights from the summit makes every step of the climb worth it.

One of the most magical experiences at the summit is watching the sunrise. Many climbers start their final ascent to the peak in the early morning, often around midnight, to arrive at Uhuru Peak by dawn. As they reach the top, the darkness begins to lift, and a soft glow fills the sky. Slowly, the sun peeks over the horizon, casting pink and golden light across the landscape. Watching the sunrise from Kilimanjaro is unforgettable because it feels like the entire world is waking up right in front of you. The colors are brilliant, and there's a magical stillness in the air as climbers gather to witness this natural spectacle. The sun lights up the sky in shades of pink, orange, and yellow, painting the mountain in warm colors that feel like a reward for the hard work of the climb.

The view also includes the icy glaciers that cap Kilimanjaro's summit. These glaciers are a reminder of the mountain's age and the power of nature. Although they are slowly melting due to climate change, the glaciers still cover parts of the summit in sparkling white ice, creating a striking contrast against the darker volcanic rock. From the top, the glaciers look like frozen rivers stretching across the landscape, their ridges and valleys catching the sunlight and sparkling like crystals. These ancient ice fields make the summit feel like a place from another world—frozen, pure, and untouched. The sight of the glaciers is particularly special because not many mountains in Africa have snow or ice, especially near the equator, so climbers feel like they are standing on something rare and precious.

Looking out from the summit, climbers can also see the clouds below, giving them the sense of standing above the world. Kilimanjaro is so high that, on many days, climbers actually look down on the cloud cover below, making it seem like they're floating in the sky. The view of the clouds from above is almost like an ocean of white, stretching out as far as the eye can see. Sometimes, there are breaks in the clouds, where climbers can glimpse the landscape far below. On clear days, you might even be able to see distant landscapes, such as the lush plains of Tanzania and even parts of Kenya. This sense of height is awe-inspiring because it's rare to experience looking down on the world in this way.

In the distance, the climbers might also see the peaks of other smaller mountains, as well as the endless savanna and forest below. Kilimanjaro's summit offers a view of different landscapes that are full of life and variety. The forests look like dark green carpets stretching out toward the horizon, while the savanna plains appear golden and vast, dotted with patches of trees and watering holes. With binoculars or a strong camera lens, some climbers can spot animals moving across the plains below. It's a reminder that Kilimanjaro sits in the heart of wild Africa, home to lions, elephants, zebras, and giraffes. From this high up, the world below seems peaceful, like a painting that captures Africa's incredible beauty and diversity.

Another unforgettable sight from the summit is Mawenzi, the second-highest peak of Kilimanjaro. Mawenzi is a rugged, spiky peak that rises up next to Kilimanjaro's main summit, creating a dramatic view of sharp rocks and deep shadows. Mawenzi Peak has its own unique look, with jagged edges and steep cliffs that add to the dramatic landscape. Although it's not as tall as Uhuru Peak, it's still an impressive sight and a reminder of Kilimanjaro's volcanic origins. Seeing Mawenzi from the summit makes climbers feel like they're on the edge of a wild, ancient land, full of mystery and history. The contrast between Uhuru Peak's smooth summit and Mawenzi's rugged shape is one of the highlights of the view, showing the different faces of Kilimanjaro.

On exceptionally clear days, climbers might even be able to see Mount Meru, another towering mountain in Tanzania, located about 70 kilometers (43 miles) from Kilimanjaro. Mount Meru rises sharply in the distance, with its own unique beauty and majesty. Seeing another mountain from the summit adds to the feeling of adventure and discovery. It's like standing on one giant mountain and looking at another across the African plains, a sight few people get to see. Mount Meru is sometimes surrounded by clouds, giving it a misty, almost magical appearance as it rises from the landscape. The sight of Meru adds another layer of beauty and wonder to the summit experience.

Standing at the summit also offers a special kind of silence and peace. After the hard work of the climb, the summit feels like a quiet, still place, where climbers can pause and take in the beauty around them. The only sounds might be the gentle wind or the crunch of snow underfoot. This peacefulness creates a sense of reflection and accomplishment, allowing climbers to feel connected to the mountain and to nature. Many climbers take a few moments to breathe in the thin, crisp air, appreciating the fact that they are standing in a place that few people in the world will ever see.

One of the most powerful parts of reaching the summit is knowing you are at the highest point in Africa, a fact that adds to the sense of awe and excitement. Looking out over the vast African landscape, climbers feel a deep sense of pride and wonder, knowing they've achieved something extraordinary. They can look in every direction and see nothing but endless landscapes, a reminder of the mountain's height and the incredible journey they've taken to get there.

For many climbers, reaching the summit of Kilimanjaro feels like the top of the world, offering views that capture the beauty, power, and mystery of Africa. The landscapes are vast, and the journey to the summit is tough, but every challenge is worth it for the experience of standing on Kilimanjaro's peak. From the sunrise and glaciers to the clouds below and distant mountains, the views from the summit are as rewarding as they are beautiful, making Kilimanjaro an unforgettable adventure.

Chapter 14: Life at the Base of the Mountain

Life at the base of Mount Kilimanjaro is bustling, lively, and full of fascinating sights, sounds, and people. This area is home to several villages where people live, work, and go about their daily routines, all with the towering mountain as a constant presence in the background. Kilimanjaro's lower slopes and surrounding areas are rich in natural resources, allowing communities here to thrive in a unique environment. The base of Kilimanjaro is also where many climbers and adventurers begin their journeys, bringing together locals and visitors from all over the world.

One of the most interesting things about life at the base of Kilimanjaro is how closely people are connected to the land. The area around Kilimanjaro is very fertile due to the volcanic soil, which is excellent for farming. As a result, agriculture is a big part of life here. Local farmers grow crops like bananas, coffee, maize (corn), beans, and even avocados, which thrive in the warm, moist climate. You'll often see small farms and fields spread out along the lower slopes, where people work from sunrise to sunset, planting, harvesting, and tending to their crops. Coffee is especially important in this area, and many people grow it as a cash crop, meaning they sell it to make money. The coffee grown here is known for its rich flavor, and it's sold not just in Tanzania but all around the world.

In addition to farming, raising animals is also common at the base of the mountain. Many families have small herds of cattle, goats, or chickens, which provide them with milk, eggs, and meat. The animals often graze in grassy areas around the villages, and it's a common sight to see young boys or girls herding goats along the paths. These animals are a valuable resource for the people here, and they are taken care of with great care and respect. Cows, in particular, are prized, and it's not uncommon for a family to measure its wealth by the number of cows it owns. The milk is used to make local dishes, and the animals also play an important role in local ceremonies and traditions.

The people who live at the base of Kilimanjaro belong to different cultural groups, with the Chagga people being one of the largest. The Chagga have lived in this region for centuries and have developed a deep connection with the mountain. They have their own language, customs, and traditional ways of life. The Chagga people are known for their strong sense of community and their hardworking nature. Family and community are extremely important to them, and you'll often see neighbors helping each other out with tasks like farming, building, or gathering supplies. They believe in taking care of each other and making sure everyone has what they need, and this sense of unity is a big part of what makes life at the base of Kilimanjaro so special.

The Chagga people also have many traditional customs that have been passed down through generations. For example, they have stories and legends about Kilimanjaro, which they believe is a sacred mountain. Some stories say that the mountain is protected by spirits, and that only those who respect it can truly understand its power and beauty. The Chagga people also celebrate various festivals and ceremonies throughout the year, marking important times in the farming calendar or celebrating family events like weddings. These ceremonies are often colorful, with traditional music, dance, and clothing that reflect their unique culture.

Life at the base of Kilimanjaro isn't just about work and tradition, though. There is also a strong spirit of hospitality and welcome in the villages here. Because Kilimanjaro attracts climbers from all around the world, the people at the base are used to meeting visitors. Many locals work in jobs related to tourism, such as guiding, cooking, or helping with transportation. Guides and porters, in particular, play a crucial role in the Kilimanjaro climbing industry. They know the mountain trails like the back of their hands and help climbers by carrying supplies, setting up camp, and even cooking meals along the route. For many guides, working on Kilimanjaro is not only a way to make a living but also a source of pride, as they help people from all over achieve their dream of reaching the summit.

The villages at the base of Kilimanjaro also have bustling markets where locals gather to buy and sell goods. These markets are filled with fresh produce, handmade crafts, colorful fabrics, and all sorts of everyday items. Visiting a local market is a great way to experience the lively atmosphere of the area, as people haggle over prices, share stories, and catch up with friends. The markets are an important part of life at the base because they provide a place for people to sell what they've grown or made and buy things they need. Markets also allow people to connect and build a sense of community, which is important in rural life.

Education is also a big part of life at the base of Kilimanjaro. In the villages, you'll find schools where children learn basic subjects like reading, math, and science. Many parents work hard to send their kids to school, hoping they will have better opportunities for the future. Some schools even teach about Kilimanjaro, sharing the history, geography, and environmental importance of the mountain. Learning about Kilimanjaro helps students understand why their home is so special and why it's important to protect it. For some kids, growing up so close to Kilimanjaro might even inspire them to become guides, scientists, or conservationists.

The natural environment at the base of Kilimanjaro is also rich in plants and animals. Many types of trees, like fig and avocado trees, grow in the fertile soil, and the air is often filled with the songs of birds. In some areas, you might even see monkeys swinging through the trees or small antelopes grazing nearby. People and wildlife coexist closely here, and locals respect the animals and the environment. Conservation is becoming more important as people realize the need to protect the forests, streams, and wildlife that make their home unique. Local organizations work to teach people about sustainable practices, so they can protect the mountain's natural beauty for future generations.

At the base of the mountain, the air is warm and often humid, creating a climate that's perfect for lush forests and farms. Unlike the cold summit, life here is comfortable, with sunny days and cool nights. People enjoy spending time outdoors, and there's a relaxed pace to life. Family and friends gather in the evenings to share meals, tell stories, and talk about the day's events. Even though life can be tough, especially during the rainy seasons when roads get muddy and crops can be damaged, there is a strong sense of resilience among the people. They know how to handle challenges and work together to overcome any difficulties that come their way.

For those who live at the base of Kilimanjaro, the mountain isn't just a beautiful landmark; it's a symbol of strength, pride, and connection. It shapes the climate, provides resources, and brings people together. The mountain is a reminder of their ancestors, who lived in this region long before modern times, and it's a source of inspiration for future generations. Life at the base of Kilimanjaro is a blend of old traditions and new opportunities, with the mountain always watching over everything. Whether they're farming, guiding climbers, or simply enjoying the view, the people at the base share a deep bond with Kilimanjaro that is as timeless as the mountain itself.

Chapter 15: How Scientists Study Kilimanjaro

Scientists from around the world are fascinated by Mount Kilimanjaro and study it to learn more about our planet's climate, geology, and ecosystems. With its towering height, glaciers, forests, and unique wildlife, Kilimanjaro is like a natural laboratory, offering clues about Earth's past and possible hints about the future. Researching Kilimanjaro isn't easy, but it's worth the effort because the mountain holds valuable secrets. From its icy summit to its lush base, Kilimanjaro provides a range of environments for scientists to explore, helping them understand everything from climate change to plant and animal adaptations.

One of the main reasons scientists are interested in Kilimanjaro is its glaciers. Kilimanjaro's glaciers are unique because they're found so close to the equator, where glaciers are rare. These glaciers have been around for thousands of years, but they are shrinking quickly due to rising global temperatures. Scientists study the glaciers to understand how climate change affects ice at high altitudes. They measure the thickness of the ice, record temperatures, and take photographs to track changes over time. Researchers also drill deep into the ice to pull out samples called ice cores, which hold tiny air bubbles trapped thousands of years ago. By examining these bubbles, scientists can learn about past climates and compare them with today's climate, giving us an idea of how fast changes are happening.

Another part of Kilimanjaro that scientists study is its weather patterns. The weather on Kilimanjaro is complex because it varies so much from the base to the summit. Scientists set up weather stations at different altitudes to measure temperature, humidity, wind speed, and precipitation. This data helps them understand how weather works in high-altitude environments and how it might be changing. For example, they study how rainfall patterns have shifted over the years, which affects both the mountain's glaciers and the plants and animals that live there. By tracking changes in weather on Kilimanjaro, scientists can gain insights into broader climate trends that might be affecting other parts of the world too.

The plants and animals on Kilimanjaro are also subjects of scientific study. Since Kilimanjaro has different climate zones, scientists can observe how plants and animals adapt to these varied conditions. For instance, they study the forests and grasslands at lower altitudes, where animals like monkeys, elephants, and antelopes live. Higher up, they explore the alpine desert zone, where only tough plants and small animals survive. Scientists examine how these plants and animals have adapted to extreme conditions, such as cold temperatures and low oxygen levels. By studying Kilimanjaro's ecosystems, researchers learn about the resilience of life and how species adapt to survive in harsh environments.

Kilimanjaro is also important for studying biodiversity. Scientists document the many different species of plants, animals, insects, and even fungi that live on the mountain. Some of these species are unique to Kilimanjaro, meaning they aren't found anywhere else on Earth. Researchers catalog these organisms to understand the diversity of life on the mountain and how it may change in the future. They look at how species interact with each other and their environment, forming a web of life. Understanding this biodiversity helps scientists predict how ecosystems might change as the climate warms or as human activities affect the area.

Geologists are another group of scientists who are drawn to Kilimanjaro because it's a dormant volcano. They study the rocks, soil, and volcanic features of the mountain to understand its geological history. By examining the layers of volcanic rock, geologists can tell when and how Kilimanjaro erupted in the past. They collect samples of lava and ash and analyze them in labs to learn more about the minerals and gases that were once inside the volcano. This research helps scientists understand how Kilimanjaro formed millions of years ago and whether it might ever become active again. Although Kilimanjaro hasn't erupted in thousands of years, studying its geology provides clues about the Earth's volcanic processes and helps us understand other volcanoes around the world.

One of the most exciting things scientists do on Kilimanjaro is fieldwork. Fieldwork means that scientists go directly to the mountain, often hiking up to remote areas to collect samples and data. Fieldwork can be challenging on Kilimanjaro because of its high altitude, steep slopes, and unpredictable weather. Researchers have to be prepared for cold temperatures and thin air, especially near the summit. They bring special equipment to measure temperature, humidity, and other factors, and they often spend days or weeks gathering information. Fieldwork on Kilimanjaro is an adventure, but it's also hard work. The data collected during field trips provides the foundation for scientific studies that help us understand the mountain better.

One area of research that is becoming more important on Kilimanjaro is conservation science. Scientists work with local communities and organizations to find ways to protect the mountain's unique environment. They study the impact of tourism, which is a major industry on Kilimanjaro, to see how it affects the ecosystem. For example, they look at how human waste, litter, and foot traffic from thousands of climbers might be harming the delicate alpine areas. Conservation scientists also examine how local agriculture affects the forests on the lower slopes, as people clear land for farming. By understanding these impacts, scientists can recommend practices that help preserve Kilimanjaro's natural beauty and biodiversity for future generations.

Technology is also helping scientists study Kilimanjaro in new ways. For instance, researchers use satellite images to monitor changes in Kilimanjaro's glaciers, vegetation, and land use over time. Satellites provide a view from above, showing areas that might be difficult to reach on foot. This technology allows scientists to track changes more easily and to compare Kilimanjaro's landscape with other mountains. Drones are also being used to capture detailed images and measure areas where glaciers are melting or where vegetation is changing. These high-tech tools help scientists study the mountain more accurately and efficiently, giving them a clearer picture of what's happening.

Some scientists also focus on the impact of climate change on Kilimanjaro. By observing how Kilimanjaro's glaciers and ecosystems are changing, researchers can make predictions about how other mountains and ecosystems around the world might be affected by warming temperatures. For example, as glaciers melt, they release water that feeds rivers and streams, supporting life in surrounding areas. If the glaciers disappear completely, it could have serious consequences for the animals, plants, and people who rely on this water. Studying Kilimanjaro helps scientists understand these complex relationships and prepare for the challenges of a changing climate.

Even with all the modern technology available, scientists also rely on the knowledge of local people to learn about Kilimanjaro. The Chagga people, who have lived near the mountain for centuries, have their own ways of understanding the land, weather, and wildlife. By talking with locals, scientists can learn about changes they have noticed over the years, such as shifts in weather patterns or animal migrations. Local knowledge helps scientists get a more complete picture of the mountain and understand changes that might not be visible from satellite images or scientific measurements alone. This collaboration between scientists and local communities is valuable because it combines traditional wisdom with modern science.

In addition to fieldwork and technology, scientists study Kilimanjaro by conducting laboratory analyses. Samples collected on the mountain, such as rocks, soil, plants, and ice, are taken back to labs where they can be analyzed in detail. In the lab, scientists can look at the chemical composition of the samples to learn about the conditions on the mountain over time. For example, they can identify minerals in rocks that reveal how the mountain formed or examine pollen grains preserved in ice to learn about ancient plant life. Lab work provides precise information that complements the observations made in the field, helping scientists piece together the history and current state of Kilimanjaro.

Overall, the scientific study of Kilimanjaro is like solving a giant puzzle. Each piece of information, whether it's an ice core, a weather reading, or a plant sample, helps scientists understand this unique mountain and its role in the larger environment. By studying Kilimanjaro, researchers learn more about how mountains are formed, how ecosystems adapt to changing conditions, and how climate change affects natural landscapes. This research is important not only for preserving Kilimanjaro itself but also for understanding our planet and finding ways to protect other ecosystems around the world. Kilimanjaro is more than just a mountain; it's a gateway to discovery, offering scientists endless opportunities to learn, explore, and uncover the mysteries of nature.

Chapter 16: The Effects of Climate Change on Kilimanjaro

Mount Kilimanjaro, with its iconic snow-capped peak and ancient glaciers, has long been a symbol of Africa's natural beauty and mystery. But in recent decades, scientists and climbers have noticed big changes happening on the mountain that point to one thing: climate change. Kilimanjaro's glaciers are shrinking, weather patterns are shifting, and the delicate ecosystems on the mountain are under stress. These changes are not only affecting Kilimanjaro itself but also the plants, animals, and even people who rely on the mountain for water, food, and shelter. By studying the effects of climate change on Kilimanjaro, scientists hope to understand how warming temperatures are impacting mountain ecosystems around the world and find ways to protect them.

One of the most noticeable signs of climate change on Kilimanjaro is the melting of its glaciers. The glaciers on Kilimanjaro have existed for thousands of years, covering the summit with glistening ice that could be seen from miles away. However, since the early 20th century, these glaciers have been steadily shrinking, and scientists have documented how they are disappearing faster than ever. This process, called glacial retreat, means that the ice is melting faster than it can be replaced by snowfall. Today, only a fraction of Kilimanjaro's original glaciers remains, and scientists estimate that if the current rate of melting continues, these glaciers could disappear completely within a few decades. Losing Kilimanjaro's glaciers would be more than just a loss of beauty; it would also mean the end of a historical climate record, as the ice holds evidence of past weather patterns and volcanic eruptions that date back thousands of years.

The temperature changes on Kilimanjaro are also a sign of climate change. Normally, temperatures on the mountain are quite cold at higher elevations, which is why ice and snow could form there even though the mountain is near the equator. But as the global climate warms, temperatures on Kilimanjaro are also rising, especially at night. This warming means that less snow falls to replace the melting ice, and the existing ice can't stay frozen as easily. Instead of being covered in ice and snow, parts of Kilimanjaro's summit have become bare rock. The higher temperatures are also affecting other parts of the mountain, causing the vegetation zones to shift upward. For instance, some plants that once only grew in the lower, warmer zones of the mountain are now found at higher altitudes as they adapt to the changing climate.

Another major impact of climate change on Kilimanjaro is the shift in rainfall patterns. Kilimanjaro's weather is influenced by winds that bring rain to its slopes, especially during the rainy seasons. This rain helps sustain the forests, grasslands, and animals that live on the mountain. But with climate change, the timing and amount of rainfall have become unpredictable. In some years, Kilimanjaro receives much less rain than usual, leading to droughts that dry out the forests and threaten the animals that rely on water sources. In other years, heavier rainfalls can cause landslides and wash away plants and soil, making it difficult for the ecosystem to recover. This unpredictability in rainfall affects the entire water cycle on Kilimanjaro, impacting everything from river flow to plant growth.

The forest ecosystems on Kilimanjaro are also facing challenges due to climate change. Kilimanjaro's forests act as natural sponges, absorbing moisture from the air and releasing it slowly to feed rivers and streams. This process provides water to the surrounding communities and helps maintain a stable climate on the mountain. However, as temperatures rise and rainfall becomes more unpredictable, these forests are under threat. The lack of consistent rainfall can weaken trees, making them more vulnerable to disease, pests, and even forest fires. When the forests suffer, it affects the entire ecosystem, as many animals depend on the forests for food and shelter.

The loss of forest cover also means that the mountain loses its ability to capture and store moisture, further worsening the water shortage in nearby areas.

In addition to changes in rainfall, scientists are observing an increase in extreme weather events on Kilimanjaro, such as intense storms and droughts. These extreme events are putting extra stress on the mountain's ecosystems, making it harder for plants and animals to survive. For example, heavy storms can cause landslides that destroy vegetation and disturb animal habitats. Droughts, on the other hand, can make food and water scarce, forcing animals to migrate or face starvation. Plants that once thrived on Kilimanjaro's slopes are struggling to survive in these harsher conditions, and some species may even face extinction if the climate continues to change at its current rate.

The wildlife on Kilimanjaro is also feeling the effects of climate change. Animals that live on Kilimanjaro have adapted to specific climate zones, and as these zones shift due to rising temperatures, animals are forced to move to new areas to find food and suitable habitats. For instance, certain birds and mammals that once lived in the forest zones might move higher up the mountain to escape the heat. However, this movement can cause competition between species that are not used to sharing the same space, leading to changes in the food chain. Some animals may struggle to find enough food in their new habitats, and others may not survive the transition at all. Climate change threatens the delicate balance of Kilimanjaro's wildlife, putting unique species at risk.

One of the most concerning effects of climate change on Kilimanjaro is the potential impact on local communities. The Chagga people and other communities near Kilimanjaro depend on the mountain's water sources for drinking, farming, and other daily needs. As glaciers melt, forests shrink, and rainfall becomes less predictable, the water supply for these communities is at risk. Droughts and reduced water flow in rivers make it harder for people to grow crops, which can lead to food shortages and increased poverty. Climate change is not just affecting the natural beauty of Kilimanjaro; it is also affecting the lives of the people who call the area home. Some local groups are working with scientists and conservation organizations to find ways to protect their water sources and adapt to the changing environment, but the challenges are significant.

Scientists are studying the effects of climate change on Kilimanjaro to better understand what is happening and how to slow down the damage. Researchers measure glacier size, track temperature changes, and monitor the health of forests and wildlife. They use this data to make predictions about how Kilimanjaro's ecosystems might change in the future and what can be done to protect them. For example, conservation projects are focusing on replanting trees in the forest zones to help restore the mountain's ability to capture and hold moisture. Scientists are also studying how different plant and animal species might adapt to changing conditions, providing insights that could help protect biodiversity on other mountains around the world.

In addition to studying Kilimanjaro, scientists are raising awareness about the importance of taking action to combat climate change. They emphasize that Kilimanjaro's melting glaciers and changing ecosystems are part of a larger global trend. If climate change continues unchecked, other mountains and natural areas could face similar problems, putting even more plants, animals, and communities at risk. By sharing their research, scientists hope to inspire people to take steps to reduce carbon emissions, protect forests, and support conservation efforts that can slow down the effects of climate change.

Some solutions to help protect Kilimanjaro involve working with local communities. Conservationists and scientists are partnering with the Chagga and other local groups to develop sustainable farming practices that use less water and protect the soil. By teaching farmers how to grow crops in ways that conserve water, these projects aim to reduce the pressure on Kilimanjaro's water sources. There are also efforts to reduce deforestation by promoting alternative sources of fuel, so that fewer trees are cut down for firewood. These initiatives not only help protect Kilimanjaro's forests but also support the livelihoods of the people who depend on the mountain.

Overall, the effects of climate change on Kilimanjaro are a reminder of how interconnected our planet is. The melting glaciers, shifting ecosystems, and challenges facing local communities show how changes in one part of the world can have ripple effects on the environment and people's lives. Kilimanjaro is more than just a mountain; it's a symbol of the impact of climate change and a call to action to protect our planet. Scientists, conservationists, and local communities are working together to understand and address these changes, but the future of Kilimanjaro depends on the actions we all take to combat climate change. By protecting this magnificent mountain, we can help ensure that its glaciers, forests, and unique wildlife survive for generations to come, allowing future adventurers to experience its beauty and learn from its history.

Chapter 17: Safeguarding the Mountain for the Future

Mount Kilimanjaro is one of the world's most unique and beautiful landmarks, and people around the globe agree that it deserves to be protected for future generations to admire and explore. Safeguarding Kilimanjaro isn't just about preserving a tall mountain; it's about caring for an ecosystem, a water source, a cultural heritage, and a symbol of natural beauty. Over time, climate change, deforestation, and tourism have all had an impact on Kilimanjaro. As a result, scientists, local communities, conservationists, and governments are working together to find solutions to keep this extraordinary mountain and its surrounding environment healthy and thriving. Protecting Kilimanjaro is a challenge, but by taking the right steps, people hope to save its beauty and resources for many generations to come.

One of the biggest challenges facing Kilimanjaro is climate change. The glaciers on its peak have been melting over the last century, and the forest zones on its slopes are seeing drier conditions. Climate change is making it harder for the mountain's plants and animals to survive, as rising temperatures shift weather patterns and reduce the amount of snow that falls on the summit. The melting glaciers are particularly concerning, as they provide valuable water for the rivers and streams that flow down the mountain, supporting both wildlife and the local communities. Without these glaciers, there may be less water for everyone who relies on it. To protect Kilimanjaro, scientists believe it is important to take global action on climate change by reducing carbon emissions, which contribute to the warming of our planet. By raising awareness and encouraging individuals and governments to cut down on fossil fuels, people hope to slow down the warming that is threatening mountains like Kilimanjaro.

Deforestation is another serious issue for Kilimanjaro. The forests on Kilimanjaro's slopes play a vital role in capturing and storing moisture, which provides fresh water to surrounding communities. These forests also provide habitat for unique wildlife, including monkeys, birds, and insects, as well as many plant species found only in this area. However, in recent years, deforestation has become a problem, as people have cut down trees to make room for farms, build homes, or use wood as fuel for cooking and heating. When trees are removed, the soil is more likely to erode, and the mountain's ability to capture water is weakened. The loss of trees also impacts local wildlife, as many animals rely on forests for shelter and food. To help address this problem, conservation groups are working to plant new trees in the deforested areas of Kilimanjaro. These reforestation projects aim to restore the forests, protect the soil, and ensure there is enough water for the people and animals that live nearby. Additionally, conservationists are encouraging people to use alternative fuels, like charcoal made from sustainable sources, instead of cutting down more trees.

Tourism has both positive and negative effects on Kilimanjaro. Thousands of people travel from all over the world to climb the mountain, bringing valuable income to the local economy. Many tourists hire guides, porters, and other workers from the nearby communities, which helps support local families and businesses. However, with so many people visiting, Kilimanjaro faces certain challenges, such as litter, soil erosion, and damage to the natural environment. Some climbers don't take care of their trash, leaving litter along the trails, which can harm plants and wildlife. Additionally, walking paths become worn down from constant use, which can make the soil loose and prone to erosion, especially during the rainy season. To address these issues, the Tanzanian government has created guidelines for responsible tourism on Kilimanjaro. These guidelines require climbers and guides to follow specific rules, such as carrying out all trash and staying on designated paths to protect the fragile environment. Some organizations have also created cleanup programs that bring volunteers to the mountain to remove litter left behind by visitors, helping keep Kilimanjaro's trails clean and safe for everyone.

Local communities, especially the Chagga people, play an essential role in safeguarding Kilimanjaro. The Chagga people have lived near the mountain for centuries and have developed a deep respect for its resources. In recent years, they have become actively involved in conservation projects to protect Kilimanjaro. For example, some Chagga farmers are participating in sustainable agriculture programs that help them grow crops without harming the environment. These programs teach farmers to use water more efficiently and avoid practices that could lead to soil erosion. By working with conservationists, the Chagga people are helping to ensure that their farms stay productive while also protecting the forests and water sources on Kilimanjaro. Many locals are also involved in ecotourism projects that allow tourists to experience the natural beauty of the mountain in a way that respects and preserves the environment.

Education is another key component in the effort to protect Kilimanjaro. Schools, organizations, and community groups are working to teach young people about the importance of conserving the mountain's resources. Programs in local schools often include lessons about climate change, deforestation, and the impact of pollution, helping students understand how these issues affect Kilimanjaro and what they can do to make a difference. By involving the next generation in conservation efforts, these programs help ensure that the knowledge and respect for Kilimanjaro's environment are passed down. Some students even participate in tree-planting days or community cleanups, learning firsthand how they can protect the mountain. This sense of responsibility encourages them to become future leaders in conservation.

Scientists and researchers are also taking important steps to safeguard Kilimanjaro by studying its ecosystems and climate. By monitoring changes in temperature, glacier size, and plant and animal populations, scientists can better understand how climate change and human activity are impacting the mountain. They use this data to make predictions about the future and recommend strategies for protecting the mountain's resources. For example, some scientists have proposed using advanced technology to measure the amount of water stored in the mountain's glaciers and forests, which could help local communities plan for periods of drought. Others are studying ways to restore native plant species that have been affected by deforestation and changing temperatures. These research efforts provide valuable information that can guide conservation policies and help protect Kilimanjaro for the future.

One innovative approach to safeguarding Kilimanjaro involves community-based conservation efforts. These projects are led by local residents and involve everyone from farmers to schoolchildren in protecting the mountain. By involving the community in conservation, these projects help people feel more connected to the mountain and more responsible for its future. Community members might organize cleanups, work on reforestation projects, or teach each other about sustainable farming techniques. Some conservation groups provide incentives, such as small grants or training, to encourage local participation in these projects. By empowering people to take action, these efforts create a sense of ownership over Kilimanjaro's resources and encourage long-term commitment to conservation.

Finally, the Tanzanian government and various international organizations are working together to create and enforce laws that protect Kilimanjaro's environment. National parks and protected areas around the mountain have specific rules designed to prevent deforestation, pollution, and damage to wildlife habitats. For instance, cutting down trees in certain parts of the mountain is strictly prohibited, and there are limits on the number of climbers allowed on the mountain each day. These regulations help control human impact and keep Kilimanjaro's ecosystems as undisturbed as possible. In addition, international organizations provide funding and support for conservation programs, bringing together resources and knowledge from around the world to help protect the mountain.

Safeguarding Kilimanjaro for the future is about finding a balance between the needs of nature, local communities, and the people who come from all over to experience its beauty. By working together, people are taking positive steps to protect the mountain's glaciers, forests, wildlife, and water sources. Every action, big or small, can make a difference. Whether it's planting a single tree, teaching a child about conservation, or supporting policies that address climate change, these efforts all contribute to a healthier Kilimanjaro. The goal is to ensure that future generations will be able to gaze up at the snow-capped peak, wander through the lush forests, and learn about the mountain's rich history and culture. Protecting Kilimanjaro is a shared responsibility, and with everyone's help, it can remain a place of wonder, adventure, and inspiration for many years to come.

Chapter 18: Wildlife Conservation on the Slopes

The slopes of Mount Kilimanjaro are home to a variety of wildlife that is as diverse and unique as the mountain itself. From elephants to monkeys, and from colorful birds to rare insects, this area is an important refuge for many creatures. But as beautiful as this ecosystem is, it faces a number of challenges that threaten its delicate balance. With issues like habitat loss, climate change, and increased human activity, the wildlife on Kilimanjaro's slopes is at risk. Because of this, conservation efforts have become essential in protecting the mountain's animals and preserving their habitats. Wildlife conservation on Kilimanjaro is a big and ongoing project that involves the efforts of local communities, scientists, government agencies, and conservation organizations from around the world. Together, they are working to protect this special area so that its unique creatures can continue to thrive.

One of the biggest threats to wildlife on Kilimanjaro is deforestation, which removes large sections of the forest that many animals depend on for shelter and food. Over the years, people living near the mountain have cut down trees to make room for farming, to build homes, or to collect firewood for cooking. While these activities help local communities survive, they also have a big impact on the animals that live in the forest. When forests are cut down, animals lose their homes and sometimes struggle to find enough food. Monkeys, birds, and even large animals like elephants depend on these trees for food and protection. Without the forests, they are forced to move to other areas, where they may not find the resources they need. To help solve this problem, conservation groups have started reforestation projects to plant new trees on Kilimanjaro's slopes. These projects help restore habitats and give animals a better chance of survival. In addition to planting new trees, conservationists are working with local communities to encourage the use of alternative fuels, which can help reduce the need to cut down more trees.

Protecting water sources is another important part of wildlife conservation on Kilimanjaro. The streams, rivers, and small lakes on the mountain provide fresh water for animals to drink, but these water sources are shrinking due to climate change and human use. Kilimanjaro's famous glaciers are melting as temperatures rise, which means less water flows down the mountain during the dry season. As the mountain's glaciers get smaller, there is less snow and ice to melt, which can reduce the amount of water available for both people and animals. Conservationists are studying the impact of this water shortage on wildlife, especially during dry periods when animals rely even more on streams and rivers. Some projects are focused on protecting these water sources by reducing pollution, encouraging careful water use, and restoring natural vegetation around water bodies to help them hold more water. By safeguarding these vital water sources, conservation efforts are helping to ensure that animals on Kilimanjaro have access to the resources they need.

Another big focus of conservation is protecting specific endangered species that live on Kilimanjaro. Some animals that call the mountain home, such as certain species of antelope and rare birds, are considered endangered, meaning their populations are small and they face a high risk of extinction. Conservationists have developed programs to help these species survive, often by creating protected areas where they can live without being disturbed. These protected zones are carefully managed so that animals can move around freely, find food, and raise their young without the threat of human activity. By monitoring the numbers of these endangered species and studying their behavior, scientists can learn more about what these animals need to survive and how to protect them best. For example, some rare bird species that only live on Kilimanjaro's slopes are monitored closely to make sure they have enough nesting sites and food sources. Conservationists also work to protect the plants that these animals depend on, making sure that the entire ecosystem remains in balance.

Education and community involvement are key to successful conservation efforts on Kilimanjaro. Many local communities near the mountain are deeply connected to the land and rely on its resources for farming and daily life. By working with these communities, conservation organizations are helping to spread awareness about the importance of protecting Kilimanjaro's wildlife. Schools near the mountain often teach students about conservation and the importance of wildlife protection. Kids learn how animals and plants depend on each other and why it's important to keep ecosystems healthy. Some students even participate in projects where they help plant trees or take part in wildlife monitoring. This education helps inspire the next generation to become stewards of the environment, encouraging them to protect the mountain for the future. Additionally, conservation groups often work with adults in the community to teach them about sustainable farming practices, alternative energy sources, and ways to protect natural resources. By involving local people, these programs make conservation a shared responsibility and help create a strong commitment to protecting Kilimanjaro's wildlife.

Anti-poaching measures are also a crucial part of conservation on Kilimanjaro. Poaching, which is the illegal hunting or capturing of animals, has been a problem in many parts of Africa, and it can threaten species on Kilimanjaro's slopes as well. Animals like elephants, which sometimes wander up the mountain, are targeted for their ivory tusks, while smaller animals might be captured for the illegal pet trade. Poaching disrupts the ecosystem and can lead to the decline of certain animal populations. To combat this, park rangers and wildlife officials patrol the mountain and surrounding areas, working to prevent illegal hunting. They use technology like cameras and tracking devices to monitor animal movements and detect any suspicious activity. These patrols help keep Kilimanjaro's animals safe and ensure that the wildlife can continue to thrive. Some conservation programs also include awareness campaigns that educate people about the negative effects of poaching, encouraging them to respect and protect the mountain's wildlife instead.

Another exciting part of wildlife conservation on Kilimanjaro is scientific research. Scientists are studying the plants and animals on the mountain to better understand their behaviors, habits, and needs. This research helps conservationists develop more effective ways to protect the ecosystem. For example, scientists might study how climate change is affecting certain plant species on Kilimanjaro's slopes. If a particular plant that animals rely on for food is declining due to warmer temperatures, scientists can work on ways to help that plant survive, such as by planting it in new areas or introducing similar plants that can provide food. Researchers also study animal populations, tracking the numbers and movements of different species to understand how they use the mountain's resources. This information is valuable because it helps conservationists create programs that address the specific needs of each species, ensuring that all animals on Kilimanjaro have the best chance of survival.

One conservation approach that has gained attention is creating wildlife corridors. These corridors are pathways that connect different habitats, allowing animals to move safely from one area to another. On Kilimanjaro, these corridors help animals find food, water, and shelter as they move up and down the slopes. By keeping certain areas free from development, conservationists create natural highways for wildlife, which helps prevent animals from becoming trapped in small, isolated areas where resources might be limited. These corridors are especially important for larger animals, like elephants, which need to travel long distances to find enough food and water. By preserving these movement paths, conservation efforts help maintain a balanced ecosystem, where animals can roam freely and find everything they need to survive.

Conservation on Kilimanjaro also includes efforts to control invasive species—plants or animals that are not native to the area and can disrupt the local ecosystem. When non-native species spread, they often compete with native plants and animals for resources, which can harm the ecosystem. On Kilimanjaro, certain invasive plant species have spread onto the slopes, taking over areas where native plants used to grow. This makes it harder for the animals that depend on native plants to find food and shelter. Conservationists work to remove these invasive plants and restore native vegetation, which helps support the animals that rely on them. By carefully managing the types of plants that grow on Kilimanjaro, conservation programs help maintain the natural balance and protect the mountain's biodiversity.

Wildlife conservation on Kilimanjaro is a complex and ongoing effort that involves many different strategies and the cooperation of various groups. From reforesting the slopes and protecting water sources to educating communities and fighting poaching, every effort contributes to preserving the unique wildlife of this incredible mountain. With everyone working together, there is hope that Kilimanjaro's animals will continue to thrive, and the mountain will remain a sanctuary for wildlife. Conservation efforts are essential not only for the animals that live there today but also for future generations who will come to Kilimanjaro to witness its natural beauty. By taking action now, people can ensure that the mountain's slopes remain a vibrant, living landscape where wildlife can flourish for years to come.

Chapter 19: Fun Facts About Kilimanjaro

Mount Kilimanjaro, Africa's tallest mountain, is full of fun and fascinating facts that make it one of the world's most amazing natural wonders. For starters, it's not just any mountain—it's the tallest free-standing mountain on Earth, meaning it's not part of any mountain range. It rises alone, towering over the plains of Tanzania with its snow-capped peak visible from miles and miles away. Kilimanjaro stands at a massive 19,341 feet (5,895 meters) above sea level, which is about as tall as four and a half Empire State Buildings stacked on top of each other! This height makes Kilimanjaro a popular destination for climbers from around the world, especially those looking to conquer the "Seven Summits" challenge, which involves reaching the tallest peak on each continent. For many people, reaching the top of Kilimanjaro is one of their biggest dreams!

One fun fact is that Kilimanjaro is actually made up of three volcanoes. That's right—Kilimanjaro isn't a single peak but a combination of three volcanic cones named Kibo, Mawenzi, and Shira. Shira is the oldest of the three and collapsed many thousands of years ago, creating a wide plateau on the mountain's western side. Mawenzi, the second-highest peak, has a rugged, craggy appearance with sharp cliffs and deep gorges, making it almost impossible to climb. And then there's Kibo, the tallest and most famous cone, where Uhuru Peak, the highest point in Africa, is located. Kibo is considered a dormant volcano, meaning it hasn't erupted in thousands of years, but it could technically erupt again someday. Imagine climbing a mountain that was once full of flowing lava and powerful eruptions! Thankfully, Kilimanjaro has been quiet for a very long time, and scientists keep a close eye on it to make sure it stays that way.

Another cool fact about Kilimanjaro is its nickname, "The Roof of Africa." This name comes from the fact that it's the tallest point on the African continent. Standing on the summit of Kilimanjaro is like standing on top of Africa itself, looking down on the vast savannas, forests, and villages far below. Climbers who reach the summit often describe feeling like they're on another planet because the landscape is so unique and the views are absolutely breathtaking. On clear days, you can see as far as Kenya to the north and the Maasai Mara plains. Imagine standing at the top and seeing the sun rise over the African plains—no wonder so many people say it's a life-changing experience!

One of the most surprising things about Kilimanjaro is its ice and snow. Even though the mountain is located just about 200 miles south of the equator, which is one of the hottest places on Earth, its summit is covered in glaciers and snow. This snowy cap is one of the mountain's most famous features, and it's a bit of a mystery, too. The snow and ice at the top are only there because of Kilimanjaro's extreme height; at such high altitudes, the temperatures are much cooler. But in recent years, scientists have noticed that Kilimanjaro's glaciers are melting quickly, and some predict they could disappear completely within the next few decades. This would be a big loss for the mountain, as the ice and snow are part of what makes Kilimanjaro so unique and beautiful. Some people are even rushing to climb the mountain just to see the glaciers before they're gone!

Kilimanjaro has a wide variety of climates and ecosystems on its slopes, making it one of the few places in the world where you can experience almost every type of natural environment in one climb. Starting at the base, there's farmland and grasslands where crops like coffee are grown. Moving up, you enter a lush rainforest full of tall trees, hanging vines, and animals like monkeys and birds. Above the rainforest, there's a moorland zone with strange plants like giant groundsels and lobelias, which look like they're from another planet. Next comes the alpine desert, where temperatures drop and vegetation becomes sparse. Finally, at the summit, there's an arctic zone with freezing temperatures, rocky terrain, and ice patches. This incredible range of climates is one reason why climbing Kilimanjaro feels like traveling through different worlds, all on the same mountain!

Another fun fact is that Kilimanjaro has inspired stories, legends, and even books. Ernest Hemingway, a famous American author, wrote a short story called "The Snows of Kilimanjaro" in 1936, which explores themes of life, regret, and adventure. His story made the mountain famous in literature, and since then, Kilimanjaro has become a symbol of mystery and exploration. Local people, like the Chagga, also have legends about the mountain. One popular story tells of a giant spirit or "mountain god" who lives on Kilimanjaro and watches over the land. Some people believe that the snow and ice on the summit are a sign of the mountain god's power. Stories like these add to the mountain's mystique, making it a place that's not only physically impressive but also rich in culture and tradition.

Kilimanjaro is also known for its unique wildlife. Because the mountain has so many different ecosystems, it's home to animals from tiny insects to large mammals. Monkeys, leopards, and antelope can be found in the forests, while birds like the Malachite Sunbird, with its shiny green feathers, flit around the moorlands. Even higher up, there are fewer animals, but climbers have reported seeing ravens and sometimes small rodents in the rocky areas near the summit. One interesting animal that lives on Kilimanjaro is the Kilimanjaro shrew, a small, mouse-like creature that's only found on this mountain. It's amazing to think that an animal has made this huge, cold mountain its only home on Earth!

Kilimanjaro's different routes for climbers each offer a unique experience, and some have their own interesting stories. For example, the Marangu Route is known as the "Coca-Cola Route" because it's one of the easier and more popular paths, often called the "tourist route." The Machame Route, nicknamed the "Whiskey Route," is more challenging and gives climbers an up-close look at the mountain's landscapes. Each route has its own highlights, and some climbers return multiple times to try them all. Choosing a route can be like choosing an adventure, with each path offering different views and levels of difficulty.

The mountain's impact on Tanzania's economy is another fun fact. Kilimanjaro is a major source of income for Tanzania because of tourism. Every year, thousands of climbers visit Tanzania with the goal of reaching Kilimanjaro's peak, and they bring business to local guides, porters, hotels, and restaurants. The guides and porters who help climbers up the mountain are incredibly skilled and are often the unsung heroes of the adventure. They carry heavy loads, set up camps, and make sure everyone stays safe during the journey. These hardworking men and women know the mountain like the back of their hand and play a huge role in making each climb a success. For many Tanzanians, working on Kilimanjaro provides a stable income and supports entire families.

A unique event that takes place on Kilimanjaro is the annual marathon held on the mountain's slopes. The Kilimanjaro Marathon is a popular event that attracts runners from around the world who want the challenge of racing on a mountain. Running on Kilimanjaro is no easy task—the air gets thinner as you go higher, and the terrain can be rough and steep. But for those who love a challenge, there's nothing quite like running with Kilimanjaro's towering peaks as your backdrop. This marathon is a fantastic example of how people interact with the mountain in creative and exciting ways, and it shows that Kilimanjaro is more than just a place to climb—it's a place for adventure, fitness, and celebration.

Another amazing thing about Kilimanjaro is that it attracts people of all ages. In fact, the mountain has seen climbers as young as seven and as old as eighty make it to the summit! While climbing Kilimanjaro is challenging and takes serious preparation, it's accessible enough that people of different skill levels can try. Kids and grandparents have both stood on Uhuru Peak, showing that it's possible to reach the top if you're determined and prepared. Kilimanjaro has a way of bringing out the adventurous spirit in people, no matter their age.

Kilimanjaro also serves as an important natural laboratory for scientists studying climate change. Because the mountain has glaciers that are melting at a rapid rate, researchers come to Kilimanjaro to study these changes up close. The data they collect helps us understand how warming temperatures are affecting not just Kilimanjaro, but also other glaciated mountains around the world. By studying Kilimanjaro's glaciers and unique ecosystems, scientists gain valuable insights into how climate change is impacting our planet, making the mountain an important place for environmental research.

Kilimanjaro is a truly remarkable mountain that's packed with amazing facts, stories, and mysteries. Whether you're interested in its height, its wildlife, its history, or the adventure of climbing it, there's something about Kilimanjaro that captures the imagination of people from all around the world.

Chapter 20: How Kids Can Help Protect Mountains

Mountains like Kilimanjaro are beautiful, important places that need protecting, and kids can play a big role in helping keep them safe! You might think that protecting a mountain is a job for scientists or adults, but every little action helps, and even kids can make a difference. Protecting mountains means looking after their plants, animals, water, and air so that these places stay healthy for years to come. By learning about nature, making smart choices, and spreading the word, kids can be powerful mountain protectors, even from far away.

One way kids can help protect mountains is by learning about them and understanding why they're special. When you know how unique a mountain like Kilimanjaro is—how it has different climate zones, rare plants, special animals, and glaciers—it's easier to understand why protecting it is so important. Knowledge is power, and by learning all about the mountain's ecosystem, you'll be better prepared to share that knowledge with others. You could read books, watch documentaries, or ask questions about mountains and their ecosystems. Every time you learn something new, you're getting closer to being a mountain protector!

Another way to help is by reducing waste, especially plastic. Mountains, like all natural places, are negatively affected by trash. When people leave litter behind on the trails or campsites, it can harm animals, damage plants, and pollute water sources. Even if you don't live near a mountain, you can still help by using less plastic in your everyday life. For example, choosing reusable water bottles, bags, and containers instead of single-use plastic items helps reduce the amount of waste that could end up in nature. Plastic takes hundreds of years to break down, so every piece that's reused or recycled makes a difference.

By creating less waste, you're helping keep mountains clean and safe for both animals and future visitors.

Taking care of water is also super important for protecting mountains. Kilimanjaro, for instance, has glaciers that provide water to the surrounding areas, but climate change is causing these glaciers to shrink. When you use water wisely at home, like turning off the tap while brushing your teeth or taking shorter showers, you're helping to conserve water. When people use less water, it puts less pressure on natural sources like rivers and lakes that feed into mountain ecosystems. Another way to protect water sources is to avoid putting chemicals or trash down the drain, as this can pollute rivers and lakes that flow into mountain areas.

Kids can also raise awareness about mountain protection by talking to their friends and family. Not everyone realizes how much mountains contribute to the environment, from providing water and oxygen to supporting rare plants and animals. When you tell others about how amazing mountains like Kilimanjaro are and why they're worth protecting, you're helping to spread an important message. You could even get creative by making posters, drawing pictures, or writing stories about mountains and sharing them at school or with friends. By using your voice, you're reminding others that mountains are valuable and that we all have a part in keeping them safe.

Another fun way to help is by joining or starting a nature club. Many schools and communities have clubs that focus on the environment, where kids can work together on activities like clean-up days, tree-planting events, or recycling projects. If there isn't one in your school, you could even suggest starting one! In a nature club, you can learn more about conservation, make friends with others who care about the planet, and work on projects that help protect nature. These clubs often work with larger environmental organizations, which means your efforts could be part of something big that reaches even farther than you might imagine.

For kids who enjoy being outdoors, following the "Leave No Trace" principles is a great way to protect mountains. "Leave No Trace" means leaving nature just as you found it, so it stays beautiful and healthy. If you ever visit a mountain or a park, make sure not to leave any trash behind and avoid picking plants or disturbing wildlife. Stay on marked trails to prevent damaging the plants or soil, and don't carve names or markings into trees or rocks. Every small action counts, and when everyone follows these guidelines, it makes a big difference. You're showing respect for nature, which helps keep mountains pristine and safe.

Being mindful of energy use at home is another way to help protect mountains. Many of the problems facing mountains, like melting glaciers, are caused by climate change, which is worsened by using too much energy from sources that release pollution. Kids can help by turning off lights, computers, and other electronics when they're not being used. Small actions, like walking or biking instead of asking for a car ride when possible, also reduce pollution and help protect nature. Every time you save energy, you're helping slow down the effects of climate change, which is important for preserving mountains like Kilimanjaro and their ecosystems.

Supporting organizations that work to protect mountains is another way kids can make a big impact. There are many groups dedicated to conserving nature, including mountain environments. You can look for organizations that plant trees, work to reduce pollution, or help protect animals and plants in mountain regions. Even a small donation, if that's something your family can do, can help these organizations with their conservation efforts. Some organizations also offer volunteer opportunities, which can be a great way to learn more and contribute directly. By supporting groups that protect mountains, you're adding to the resources and efforts that go into preserving these special places.

Kids can also use social media and digital platforms to make a difference. If you have a safe space online where you can share your thoughts, you could post about mountain protection or share interesting facts about Kilimanjaro and other mountains. Some kids even start their own blogs or YouTube channels to talk about environmental issues. Using these platforms to spread awareness can inspire others to care about mountain protection, too. The more people know about the importance of mountains, the more they'll want to help. Just remember to always be safe online and ask an adult before sharing anything on social media.

Planting trees and learning about reforestation is another great way to protect mountains. Trees help prevent soil erosion and provide homes for animals. They also play a big role in keeping our air clean by absorbing carbon dioxide and releasing oxygen. Even if you're planting trees far from a mountain, it still helps the environment as a whole, which benefits mountain ecosystems too. Many organizations offer tree-planting programs where you can plant trees locally or even donate to plant trees in areas that need reforestation. This is a simple but powerful way to contribute to a healthier planet.

If you're a creative person, you could also use art, writing, or other talents to support mountain conservation. You could write a poem or story about Kilimanjaro, draw pictures of the mountain and its animals, or even make a video about why mountains matter. Many kids use their talents to raise awareness about the environment in creative ways. Sometimes these works of art or stories can be shared at school, in local art shows, or even online, reaching a wider audience. Using creativity to express your love for mountains can inspire others to care as well.

Finally, caring for all of nature in your daily life is one of the best ways to protect mountains, even if you live far from one. Mountains are connected to rivers, forests, oceans, and even the air we breathe. By showing kindness to nature, whether it's a local park, a garden, or just your backyard, you're supporting the larger natural world that mountains depend on. Treating animals with respect, keeping your surroundings clean, and appreciating the beauty of nature are all ways to become a guardian of the earth.

    Mountains are wonderful, unique places that give us clean water, beautiful views, rare animals, and much more. And while protecting them might sound like a big task, small steps can add up to make a big difference. When kids take action, no matter how small, they're showing the world that they care about nature and that they want a healthy planet for the future. So, keep learning, caring, and acting, and you'll be helping to protect mountains and all their amazing life for years to come.

Epilogue

You've reached the end of our incredible journey up, around, and beyond Mount Kilimanjaro! We've explored its towering heights, learned about its amazing animals and plants, uncovered the stories of early explorers, and even peeked into the science that helps protect this grand mountain. Mount Kilimanjaro is truly a natural treasure, not just for Africa, but for the whole world.

But remember, the story of Kilimanjaro doesn't stop here. It continues to change with every sunrise, with every brave climber who reaches its summit, and with every effort to keep its beauty alive for future generations. Whether you see it as a place of adventure, a symbol of nature's power, or a reminder of the importance of protecting our planet, Kilimanjaro holds lessons that go beyond its peaks and trails.

Now, it's up to you to carry what you've learned into your world. Maybe you'll tell your friends all about the wonders of Kilimanjaro or think about ways to help protect other amazing places on Earth. Who knows? One day, you might even visit Kilimanjaro and see its magic with your own eyes!

Thank you for being part of this adventure. Keep exploring, keep protecting, and always be curious about the wonders that our world has to offer. The story of Mount Kilimanjaro, and your own adventures, is just beginning.

The End.